THE BALTI

A SCHEDULED TRIBE OF JAMMU AND KASHMIR

THE BALTI

A SCHEDULED TRIBE OF JAMMU AND KASHMIR

B.R.RIZVI

GYAN

GYAN PUBLISHING HOUSE

NEW DELHI-110 002

ISBN : 9788121204026

Published in 1993 by
Gyan Publishing House
5, Ansari Road
New Delhi-110002

Composed by Computer Bureau B-3, Arjun Nagar, Delhi-51, and printed at Goyal Offset Works, Delhi

Dedicated to my late parents :

SAIYIDA AIMAN BIBI

and

SAIYID MAHDI HASAN

FOREWORD

Traditionally, the Baltis are believed to be descendants of Celtic communities settled in Scandinavia. When the water level in the Baltic Sea rose and inundated their arable lands, they were forced to flee from the area. Even after the flood subsided, the land appeared to be unusable for agriculture, having been heavily saturated with mineral salts. Migration started in many directions. The Baltis of Laddakh are related to many other communities in Kazakhstan, Russia and the Ukraine.

The highlands at the approaches of the Korakoram pass, inhabited by former Buddhists converted to Shi 'ite Islam by Mir Shamsuddin Iraqi around the turn of the 16th century, are currently receiving great attention from the news media. The present-day dispute over Kashmir may be an indication that Asia is going back to its land-based trade activities that were terminated in the 16th century.

In case such trade boom were to happen, the Balti living under Indian and Pakistani rules would be immersed in merchantile wealth as they were between the 14th and 16th centuries when they had an independent kingdom with its capital city in Skardo. Mir Samsuddin Iraqi was a saint who initiated them to the Shia faith of the Safawid Iran which held an important position on the Silk Route. What made Baltistan unique was its carvan connection with the sub-continent and, therefore, with the whole of the Spice Route.

Baltis are marginal in every way: Pakistan sees them as Shi'ite heretics; in the eyes of a mainstream Hindu they are Buddhist outcasts; for Tibetans they Moslems .... May be the Shi'ite movements in Iran and Iraq are extending the only friendly hands to them.

Nevertheless, the Baltis are also unique insofar as they constitute communities where Shi'ites and Buddhists coexist. One is filled with admiration for this type of a "postmodern" tolerance in which Islam exists as a spiritual guidance for the individual and not as a monopolizing state doctrine. One wonders if this is the true and original character of Shi'ism or, are the Baltis also marginal as Shi'ites?

One thing is certain, the Balti pehnomenon could only happen in the Indian climate of social integration. India is the country on earth with the second largest population of Moslems. The Moslems of India are opposed to the idea of a religious state. The Shi'ites, although a minority among the Moslems of India, are the spearheading element in this secularist policy.

The Balti phenomenon could be advertised throughout the world as an epitomy of India as an integrated society based on tolerance. The Buddhist festival held yearly at the monastery of Kushak Narichang in Zanskar with the assistance of the Shi'ites of Wakha could be turned into an international feast of peace and tolerance.

Social darwinism's dogmatic face is being more and more exposed as we proceed toward the 21st century. The beliefs of mankind are great values as long as they are not viewed through the linear hierarchies of evolutionism. No faith can be more celestial than another faith. No faith can claim a monopoly over "righteous path...." A society where the missionaries of a certain ideology would have been 100 per cent successful would be a very dull one. India is an important leader in World Islam. Islam needs India and India needs Islam. When Asia will rise from a long sleep, maybe the Silk Route and the Spice Route will be renamed Peace Route and Tolerance Route.

Dr. Baqar Raza Rizvi's careful documentation of the Baltis in Kargil is likely to lay the foundations of a series of scholarly research on this community. Rizvi's work is to be complimented for its comprehensive data and insight in concepts.

DR. AHMET YURUR

Professor of Ethnomusicology,
Hacettepe University
Ankara,
TURKEY

PREFACE

Ladakh has attracted attention of many a scholars, travellers and administrators but very few studies have been carried out in ethnographic depth. Kargil region remains almost unnoticed excepting a pioneering but less known of Maulvi Hashmatullah's 'Mukhtasar Tarikh-e-Jammu' written in Urdu. The present book serves to fill up this information gap by studying a lesser known tribe of Kargil and Laddakh viz., the Balti-the inhabitants of Baltistan. Their economic organization, social structure, religious organization and political organization have been studied in depth. An effort has been made to portray the mechanism of change in the above spheres. The Balti culture has been shown as an adaptive mechanism and the consequences of three successive wars as reflected on the society have also been dealt with.

Many individuals have helped me to make my present work see the light of the day. First and foremost I would express my gratitude to Dr. K.S.Singh, I.A.S., Director General, Anthropological Survey of India, who showed keen interest in this work at all stages. Dr. R.S.Mann, Deputy Director, Anthropological Survey of India, too helped me by offering his comments from time to time. I feel obliged to him. Mr. K.Ravi, Dr. A.V.Arkeri and Mr. Rafiq Haider owe my thanks for going through the manuscript, preparing bibliography and the glossary. Ms. Mamta Nautiyal took the pains of typing the manuscript very painstakingly. She too deserves my thanks.

I would express my gratitude also to my sister, Mrs. Mehar Bano, an official of Jammu and Kashmir Civil Services, Srinagar who extended her ungrudging assistance during the progress of this work. I am also thankful to my friends Mr.S.A.S.Rizvi, I.A.S.,and Ms. Janet Rizvi for their assistance and cooperation. It will be an act of ingratitude if I fail to mention the love and affection shown to me, their 'Agha Razvi', by the people of Hardas, Karkitchoo and Wakha. My special thanks are due to the then Brigadier R.S.Dyal, Brigade-Major Goyal and Captain Pant of Indian Army posted in Kargil at the time of this study who not only extended all possible help but also showered in me the best possible hospitality true to the great traditions of Indian Army. Words fail to express my feelings of gratitude ; it is only the lingering memory of the acts of kindness shown by various individuals which is my everlasting asset. Finally I would like to thank my late brother Mr. S. Abbas Husaini who showed his keen inquisitiveness in the present work until he breathed his last .

Dehradun B.R. RIZVI

CONTENTS

CHAPTER I

INTRODUCTION

The social purpose and meaning of sociological researches in India has by and large helped to enrich the coffers of epistemology more avidly than accruing any substantial benefit to the people who have been left out in a lurch-far removed from the centre-stage. Now, the objects of sociological research, the people, too demand their share in terms of benefits accrued to them as a result of such researches. How long can we ignore to see the writing on the wall ? Insulated impericism is responsible to have opiated the social scientists into the state of hypnopaedia. Their slumber remains unperturbed even if the next house in the neighbourhood is on fire. The need of the day is to come out of the shackles of epistemology and concentrate on the needs and aspirations of the people who otherwise will make it difficult for the social scientists to operate in the field of social research. Social science research in India has hardly been instrumental in accruing any benefit to the people who have been made the subject of research. The people must get precedence over epistemology. India is steeped deep into illiteracy, poverty, communalism, socio-economic inequality and physical disabilities. If the social scientists in India close their eyes to the burning problem facing the nation they will have to redefine the utility, meaning and purpose of their ivory-tower epistemology. This author therefore, pleads guilty of getting transformed from a cultural antoropologist to an ethno-journalist because he gives precedence to the people over epistemology.

Objectives :

North Western Himalayan border is the habitat of numerous communities both tribal and peasant which have attracted the attention of few researchers. There are hardly any anthropological studies available on the area and the people. The existing body of information consists mainly of the accounts of missionaries and administrators. Besides the problem of inadequate coverage, many communities remain unexplored. It is therefore, essential that this area of strategic significance to the nation is to be thoroughly studied in order to utilize the relevant information thus obtained on socio-economic life and trends of change for the welfare of these people.

This study keeping in view the above objective, initiated a comprehensive coverage of an heitherto unknown tribe of Jammu and Kashmir, the Balti with special emphases on : i) ecological adaptation to the pecular Himalayan environment presuming that the geographical conditions prevailing the region result into a distinguished culture profile vis-a-vis the plain dwelling societies; ii) Socio-cultural implications of location : border villages are located not only on a frontier of nation and civilization, i.e., India, but are also in between nations and civilizations. Naturally, the border communities were traditionally in socio-cultural interaction with the communities living across the border. After the emergence of new autonomous states consequent to decolonisation of the area these ties received a set back and ultimately got snapped. Therefore, it will not be out of interest to see the nature and extent of such linkages maintained by the Balti with their counterparts living across the border in other countries; and iii) trends of socio-economic changes since independence that resulted into extension of administration into the remote villages of the border region such as spread of education, network of roads, community development and family welfare programmes etc. This study keeping 1947 as a base line will make an attempt to go into the details of process and mechanism of change and its cumulative effect on the traditional life of the people.

Method of study :

In an area study the traditional approach of making a particular community as the main focus of enquiry may fail to present a clear picture of the regional patterns and of the changing situation. Hence, two multi-ethnic villages of Kargil viz. Hardas and Wakha were made the major foci of intensive investigations.

Hardas :

Hardas "the green meadow" is a village situated over the left bank of the mighty Dras river. The outline of the village is an alongated strip that runs parallelly with the river. The village is situated about 3 kms west of Kargil, the eastern flank is situated on the confluence of Drass, Suru and Wakha rivers. The old Srinagar-Skardo Road passes through the village. Hardas is situated at 9,350 ft. above the mean sea level and at latitude of 30° 4' and longitude 76° 10'

The village is predominantly inhabited by the Balti. There are six Kashmiri families who are referred as Khachepa and are the descendants of a Kashmiri soldier accompanying the great Dogra general Zorawar Singh to Kargil and later settled down at Hardas. Subsequently, he married with a Balti woman. Another family is headed by a former Bodh from Leh, who, after embracing Islam, married with a village girl and settled down in the village.

The village finds a mention in the famous book of Cunningham on Ladakh (1853, reprint 1970) wherein he "felt particularly struck .... with the bold ingenuity displayed in the equiduct of .... Hardas."

The village is situated about one hundred feet above the level of Dras river. In absence of any lift irrigation devices this mighty torrent remains practically untapped. However, during the winters when the aguaduct (*kuhl*), which is the only source of water supply to the village, gets frozen, the villagers bore small holes on the solid icy surface of the river in order to tap drinking water.

Hardas consists of five hamlets. From west to east they are : Soz-buthanng, Gopi-thang, Gon, Thang and Gronjug. The etymology of the hamlets is unknown. 'Thang' however, is a term for flat plains such as the famous Chang-thang in eastern Ladakh, known after the Champa nomad. The village possesses two mosques and a *matamsara.*

According to Gazetteer of Kashmir and Laddakh (1890) there were 14 households in the village. Now there are 82 households in Hardas with a total population of 543:195 male and 248 females.

Hardas is famous for its apricot (*chuli*) orchards. The villagers said it with a sense of pride that their ancestors brought the seeds from Skardo and planted them at Hardas. During the autumn the village runs riot with golden apricots (*chuli*) with a tinge of vermillion. Besides, apricots apples and mulberries are also grown in plenty.

Wakha :

Embedded in a resplendent green valley and dominated by the ruins of the formidable Wakha fort and a hilly feature-the kind Mary holding a child in her arm (*zar-zar-broq*) resembling looking at the village like a ageless Sphinx, the village Wakha derives its name from the river that divides it into two halves. Wakha is situated 8 Kms west of Nameik-la at a height of 11,000 ft. above the mean sea level. Jonaraja refers this village as a place where a battle was ensued between Vakatanyas (the people of Wakha) and Kalmanyas(the Balti of Kharmang). The Gazetteer (Ibid). shows 40 households in the village. In 1975 there were 130 households with a population of 893:469 males and 424 females. Out of 130 households 66 households with a population of 530 belonged to Bodhs and 64 households with a population of 365 were of Muslims. The villagers reportedly traced their descent from one Kunchoq Sharaftan who came and settled down at Wakha from Purang. With him came his two sons Lobzong Gyalpo and Tumber Gualpo. Once the two brothers chased a wild goat in the Wakha forest. Tumber Gyalpo saw the creature standing still with a tuft of grass in its mouth looking at him with its impleading tearfilled eyes: He took a pity on it and went away. Later he became a famous monk- reincarnate Kushak Narichang: and migrated to Zanskar and built a monastery there. His brother Lobzong took the reigns of the Kingdom and gave many rulers to Kargil : as his eldest son Singye'Gyalpo became the king of Phokar, the next son Chogyal Gyalpo became the king of Stakche: his third son Khri Sultan became the king of Wakha and Kartse, the next son Zirgoo Rgycho, died issueless. The then Numberdar of Wakha Male Khan traced his descent from the youngest son of Lobzong Gyalpo whose name was Rgyaldecho. He was in the 11th descending generation of Kunchoq Sharaften.

The village constituted of 8 hamlets viz. (i) Se Broq or Zer- broq, (ii) Rgyalkhan, (iii) Chiskortse, (iv) Goma Broq, (v) Broq- Dantse, (vi) Ya-khang, (vii) Gyanchoqs and (viii) Phret bu-Muslim and Buddhists live together in all the hamlets of the village where in mosques and monasteries exist side by side ; a monastery can be easily recognised by the prayer flags and a row of small temples (Lha-Khang) whereas a mosque can be easily identified through its peculiar architecture and minarets. The *Jama Masiid* of the village is, situated near the ruins of Wakha fort. It was reportedly built by Babar Khan, the youngest son of Lobzong Rgyaldecho ; who, provided rulers to Wakha. It is said that Gyaldecho was issueless. The Lamas told him that if he agrees to give his son to Islam, he will be blessed with one. Rygaldecho agreed to do so. A son was born and was converted to be a Muslim. He was named Babar Khan, who invited a preacher from Zaddibal (Kashmir) for preaching and leading the prayers in the village mosque. Babar Khan's grand son was Hashim Khan. It is during his kingdom that Zorawar Singh made incursion in Kargil, captured Hashim Khan and externed him to Leh where he died after some time.

The main monastery of the village is situated in the centre of the village. It is a recently built structure of 18 square ft on the ruins of the old monestery which was reportedly burnt and razed to ground allegedly by Zorawar Singh.

Field Work :

The field work was completed in seven months in two spells of five months and two months each in the years 1973-75. Conventional tools of anthropological research were used during the study viz., interviews, genealogical method, case study method and participant observation.

Establishment of Rapport :

Here I would like to compliment the soldiers of Indian Army posted at Kargil and at the Brigade office. My first task was to establish my identity and create confidence in the hearts of ever vigilant officers of Indian Army.Brigadier R.S.Dyal, the Brigade Major and other officers of Brigade office in Kargil were extremely hospitable and polite but at the same time very firm in not allowing me to enter into the 'Inner Lines' without satisfying themselves about my credentials. Although I was issued a permit by the Ministry of Defence; even then whenever I would go to seek permission to enter into the inner lines the army officers would lose no time in giving a ring to officer's mess asking for sizzling pakoras and tea and then they would seek an excuse with a smiling face requesting me to come once again. I was losing my patience fast as no news came from Army Headquarters until one day when I was invited by the Brigadier, who extended the permission and all necessary assistance in course of the field work.

I entered in Hardas accompanied by Army officers. My first halt was at *matamasara* of the village where I requested the people who assembled there to inform the village Numbardar. Before the Numbardar arrived, a young priest with a white robe approached me. He wanted to know the purpose of my visit. He asked my name. When I replied, 'I am Rizvi', he asked whether Rizvi was my name or title (surname). When I informed that I am, one of the descendants of Imam-e-Raza, hence Rizvi, the priest took me into a tight embrace. I thanked my army escorts and requested them to convey to Brigade office my safe arrival to Hardas. The priest Sheikh Hasan instructed the villagers to make arrangements for my stay in his sitting room which was decorated in the peculiar Central Asian style. A sitting room with a huge persian carpet equipped with a number of cylindrical pillows (*gao-takia*) was offered to me. This room became a rendezevous in the next thirty days. *Qahwa* was served in tiny glass tumblers (*finjaan*) accompanied with the fresh ripe golden apricots. Soon came Haji Mehdi, the Numbardar of the village and Haji Ghulam, the father of Sheikh Hasan.

The tone of work was set by a brief talk delivered by me about the objectives of my visit to the village. Seeing a transistorised radio-set in my possession some elders could not resist their temptation to listen the Balti programme aired by Radio Muzaffarabad. I started pondering over the limitations of our own national communication net work. Could not India provide a Balti Programme to the people from Radio Leh? Why this communication gap was allowed to exist resulting into isolation of the people with the mainstream of Indian culture and civilization ?

Next day I visited Agha Mehdi, an elderly figure in late seventies with a huge flowing beard of golden hue. His ancestors were brought from Kharmang to guide the people to Islamic ways and lead the prayers in the village mosque. Agha Mahdi's sole occupation was to imbibe theological learning among the villagers. His two sons, already married, were living separately. The Agha do not own lands of their own and eke out their livelihood from *male-saadat* portion of *khums* levy paid regularly by the villagers. Agha Mahdi could not converse in Urdu. Through an interpreter he conveyed his feelings to me, : "You, the descendant of the Prophet, have honoured me by paying a visit to my house. I am a poor man and thus unable to extend due hospitalities to you. Please accept a humble gift from me," and then he beckoned to a big cock lurking around. The village children chased the poor bird all around,caught it and brought to me. I was speechless due to embrassment and too overwhelmed too speak. I tried to resist to take away one of the very few precious birds that Agha Mahdi was having in his courtyard but all my pleadings went unheeded. Agha Mahdi instructed the interpreter to take the bird to my camp. No sooner I would enter in any house in Kargil, I would invariably be served with brackish tea, boiled eggs, and leavened cakes of barley or the flour of parched *grim'*.

It was a sunny but extremely cool afternoon of August 10,1973. I was sitting in his camp with a gathering of village elders enjoying myself with fresh ripe apricots. One person was breaking hard stones extracting its soft and sweet Kernal. The villagers believed that the Kernal of apricot seeds is a cure for many ills besides an antidote for the side effects of fresh apricots. While I was busy in a group interview I heard a banging sound. One of the villagers quipped, a *lattoo* (mine) has got exploded", another participant got up with an anxious face and went out of the room saying. "Sultan had gone with supplies". He was the anxious father of Sultan. Around 7.30 P.M. Sheikh Hasan informed me that Sultan has been grievously injured in the mine blast and has been brought to the Military

Hospital, Kargil. Sultan died the same night. All efforts to save his life proved futile. His body was brought to the village in the midnight and was put in the western verandah of *matamsara* for funeral bath. I could recollect, Sultan was an extremely handsome lad of 16 or 17 years who used to bring milk to my camp everyday.

On the next morning, the whole village was assembled in *matamsara*. The body sans left foot, had a big gaping hole on the chest. The missing leg flew into scores of pieces by the impact of the explosion. Sheikh Hasan and the Akhun of Hardas supervised the funeral bath and the body was laid to rest in a grave situated in the compound of the *Matamsara*. The burial was preceded by the recitation of dirges in Balti narrating the martyrdom of Hazrat Ali Akbar, the 18 year old son of Imam Husain in Karbala. The funerary prayers (*namaz-e-janaaza*) were held for bringing solace to the soul of the deceased. The hearth of the house where the death had occurred remained silent on the day of funeral. The members of the lineage supplied cooked mutton, paste of parched *grim* flour *(Khacha)*, barley cakes and tea to the house of the deceased.

On the third day each family of the village sent 3kgs. of *Khacha* and 250 gms of butter besides making their offering at the grave of the deceased. The offerings made at the grave were pooled for distribution among the deserving orphans and widows of the village having no source of livelihood. I too sent about 5 kgs. of rice to the deceased's family as my humble contribution, which was thankfully acknowledged by the deceased's father.

Having passed 30 days, I returned to Kargil with a heavy heart. The affection and esteem with which I was treated in Hardas is beyond description. The Brigadier at Kargil further suggested to me to see an ethnic group viz., Broq Bodh living in the Indus Valley near Batalic region. He was of the view that the Broq Bodh are from Kullu region of Himachal Pradesh as their caps are similar to those of Kullu caps. A '3-tonner', was provided to take me from brigade office to 'Interior' from where another vehicle took me to Batalic. I reached Batalic in the evening and was lodged in the officer's apartment . Next day three ponies were arranged by Army officials for transporting the luggage to Garkoon, the destination, 11 kms. away from Batalik. I started my journey along the left bank of the mighty Indus. The loud torrent seemed as if thousands of mines were exploding simultaneously. Cholichen, the first village inhabited by the Broq Bodhs was passed. Reaching near Garkoon one had to cross a rickety wooden bridge on the Indus which (shook) even with a strong gust of wind. I crossed the shaky bridge slowly holding my breaths and found myself at the getaway of Garkoon. Garkoon is a village of grape-vines and white apricots' (*Karpochuli*). The rows of *Chorten* and *mani* walls were littered with the stone pebbles inscribed with "Om, Mani, Padma, Om". Garkoon struck me with its elaborate flowerbedsin which the Dok-Pa grow flowers for decorating their headgears. Entering into the village I came across with a group of women busy in breaking stones of apricot seeds. I asked them through my interpreter whether I could get a place to stay. A lady got up and told me in chaste Urdu, "I am Ganskit Dolma, the wife of Chetan Paljore. My husband has just retired from Laddakh Scouts. Sahib ! You can stay in my house. All officers stay in my house. My house is very good". She did not exaggerate. The room was tastefully decorated with a huge carpet bearing a dragon motif. The beauty of the room was added by small windows opened into a hush green meadow intersected by the Indus. The wooden panels of the windows were tastefully decorated with tinted coloured glass pieces.

Garkoon is predominantly inhabited by the Buddhist Dard migrated from Gilgit. How a pocket of Buddhism could survive the waves of Islamic onslaught is still a mystery to me. The dialect spoken by the people is slightly different from Shina and has been referred to as Bros-khat by Grierson in Linguistic Survey of India but it is known as Bros-pot in Garkoon. Ganskit, in her middle forties, was issueless though she was extremely eager to have an issue. Off and on she would extend her palm before me in order to have an idea as how many children she was going to bear. Invariably the answer to her query would be "six" and her face would lit up with a bright smile. Dolma enjoyed all amenities of modern living: 'Yera' tumblers, a pressure stove, a transistorised radio-set and a 'Hawkins' pressure cooker. Chetan Paljore, in his mid fifties was equally amiable, and very proud of his medals that he won during 1965 action. His most proud possession was an empty half of a shell which he used as grinding stone. Cooking of mutton was his first love.

Since the scope of the present study did not allow me to study the Bodh in details, I had to remain content with the collection of a few very interesting case studies shedding light on conversion from Islam to Buddhism and vice-versa.

Having spent nearly ten day at Garkoon I returned to Kargil on way back to Dehradun.

I could not proceed to Kargil in 1974 due to my indisposition to be followed by my marriage. However, I availed the opportunity in 1975. This time I came with a team consisting of 3 physical anthropologists and a statistical assistant. The physical anthropologists were interested in studying certain demo-genetic aspects of the people of Laddakh and Kashmir.

Now, I was in search of a village where Buddhists and Muslim population are more or less equally divided. Though it was a difficult choice but I knew it fully well from my earlier experience in Kargil that as one moves towards east, the Muslim population becomes thinner and thinner. With Dr. R.S. Negi, the then Superintending Anthropologist, I drove in search of the destination one afternoon. We drove past the first village Shargola as there were very few Buddhist families in that village; than came Mulbekh characterised with a dominating idol of Maitraiya honed from a single rock. There were only a few Muslim families at Mulbekh, however some knowledgeable persons of Mulbekh informed that the next village Wakha will be an ideal village from my point of view and it was! By the time we reached Wakha, the sun had already gone behind the impenetrable Himalayan peaks. I requested Dr. Negi to return to Kargil as it was very risky to travel on a hilly road after the dusk. I was left alone on the road side with three steal trunks and a bedding. A few inquisitive faces gathered round me and were told about the purpose of my visit and were also asked for a place to stay. One of them, Fida Hussain took me to his house which was situated at a considerable height, and offerred aroom in his newly built house. Here again the first task of filling up of house-hold census schedules by going door to door did not only help to collect accurate data but also it was the beginning of establishment of rapport with the villagers.

Each household census schedule was treated as an exhaustive family record incorporating entries on death, divorces, desertions, and many other important characteristic of the family concerned. This time my interpreter was Maley Khan, the Numbardar of the village, though a controversial figure among the Muslims but a picture of tolerance and secularism, his case study provides an insight as how the Buddhists and Muslims have been able to live together in harmony for the last four centuries. After living 20 days in Fida Hussain's hospitable house I shifted to a nearby house that belonged to a Buddhist. In Wakha I could see the nature and process of interaction between two diametrically opposite religious traditions; Buddhism on one hand, partly animistic and wholly polytheistic and polyandrous and Islam, on the other hand, an irrefutably monotheistic and largely monogamous with mild traces of polygyny.

CHAPTER II

SETTING

The Area :

Kargil derives its name from its ecological setting. In Bodhi, the term Kar stands for 'White' and '*Gil* or *Geil*' for 'Curves'. Hence, the term' white curves' denotes the curve of the Himalayan peaks completely devoid of any form of vegetation excepting perhaps the sparsely scattered growth of wild juniper bushes. Green patches of grass however, offer a pleasant surprise to the eyes otherwise tired of seeing the brown and barren vastness of the Himalayan peaks. The climate is generally dry in summer but arctic in winter when mercury dips down below the freezing point-a minus seventeen degree celcius at Dras.

Kargil is named after its administrative headquarters situated in a village of the similar name. Hashmatullah (1939 :680) reports: once upon a time a vast lake was formed by Indus that started from Kachora situated in Baltishtan and touched Khalsi. The lake started drying up gradually and consequently green patches appeared which attracted the pastoral Aryan hordes of Central Asia whose population was extended upto Gilgit and Astor. First these people settled down in the upper Indus Valley with their herds. Gradually their population occupied Purig and Baltistan where they are known as Broq-pa or Droq-pa. Later the populations of the Dardie origin were replaced by the Balti hordes.

The traditional name of Kargil is *purig* or *purik* which appears to many a knowledgeable persons of the area, to be a derivation from the term '*potriksha*' or the 'people of pot'. The local traditions indicate that the Dards were in complete control of Kargil and adjacent areas including Leh till 300 B.C. It is said that a Mongoloid King Neistheldon attacked Laddakh. captured Zanskar and subsequently extended his sovereignty upto Nameik-pass. He built a fort at a palace known as Phokar near

Shargola village and extended his rule westward upto Dras. Hence, the entire area from the west of Nameik (la) pass to the east of Zo-ji-la came under the rule of Neistheldon, referred also as *Pot-riksha* which later came to be known as Purik or Purig. Kargil now consists of the valleys formed by Dras, Suru and Wakha rivers, which are the tributaries of the mighty Indus river. The river banks are occupied by flourishing hamlets surrounded by willow and Poplar groves. The area is relatively moderate in climate as a greater force of sun and warmth in summer helps the growth of vegetation. Wheat, grim and barley flourish but orchards are few.

Kargil, declared as a district in 1979 now consists of two sub divisions viz., Zanskar and Kargil. It is bordered in west with Barumulla, Srinagar and Anantnag districts of Kashmir. In east with Leh, in north with Gilgit and in south with Lahul-Spitidistrict of Himachal Pradesh. Most of the villages in Kargil are situated at a height of 11,000 ft. above the sea level. The average rainfall per year is 25.172". Kargil's population lives in villages of the varying population size : 33.00 per cent of Kargils population lives in smaller villages of less than 200 hundred population. In 45.00 per cent villages population varies between 200 to 499; bigger villages in the population range of 500-999 accommodate 1.00 per cent of the population whereas only 3.00 per cent population lives in village with 1000-1999 population size (Census of India : 1961).

Kargil has acquired a strategic significance due to its geographical setting. It is more or less equidistant from the capital cities of Kashmir, Baltistan and Laddakh. Its effective linkage with Punjab through Jammu, and Himachal Pradesh and also with Central Asia via Leh, Yarkand and Kashghar made it a bustling centre for trade and commerce. The legendry gold mines of the Mount Kailash, the world famous *pasham* of Changthang, the Chiness silk rustling in from the east; tea, salt, borax and spices from the west passed through the brittle tracks of Kargil and thus, igniting the aspirations of the many a medieval rulers who scrambled with one another not only to annex Kargil in their kingdoms but also to have an effective control over all the routes emanating from it. Armies, traders, and missionaries from China, Central Asia, Middle East and Europe treaded on the treacherous routes of Kargil with their varying ambitions from the time immemorial. Thus, Kargil emerged as a converging point of a many a civilizations, ethnic groups and faiths.

Argons, e.g., may be cited as a case. They are the descendant of Muslim traders of Yarkand and kashghar and the local Laddakhi women with whom the former married and lived with during prolonged winters when the Korakoram pass would remain closed due to heavy snowfall.

Ethnic History

The ethnic history of Kargil is enveloped in a thick blanket of darkness but the local traditions suggest that the earliest settlers in Kargil were Mons, a North Indian tribe and Laddakh, according to Hashmatullah (Ibid.680) was known as Mon-yul(The country of the Mons). It is during this period that two persons from the same stock Tisuk and Khungsuk came with their people in the lower Indus Valley and laid the foundation of Chigten.

The Mon were displaced by the Dards. According to Francke (1926:23) the entire Laddakh was inhabited by Dards at one point of time. He had found three skulls in four ancient Dard graves whose cephalic indices varied between 74 to 77. He is of the opinion that the people who built the ancient graves were probably of Dard stock. I have already described the legends connected with the origin of Dards and their distribution of population in the area. The Dards, as said earlier were displaced by the more powerful Mongoloids from the east and laid the territorial foundation of Purig or Kargil around 300 B.C.. The Dard settlements were later shifted to the safer highlands of Laddakh by virtue of which they earned the identity-Brogpa or 'high landers'.

In the Suru Valley the first migrants are stated to be Dards from Gilgit who built the Lonchey Khar fort. Their population gradually occupied the whole of Suru valley. Similarly, Dard colonies were gradually established at Phokar, Wakha, Dah, Darchik, Silmo, Hano, Cholichan, and Lalung. The Gilgit immigrants settled down in different valleys and got organised into smaller and independent socio-political units. The Mongolian King Neistheldon weilded these small socio-political units into a state ruled by subsequent Buddhist Kings until Zorawar Singh annexed Kargil and included it in the Dogra Kingdom.

MATERIAL CULTURE

The material culture in Kargil is the product of the ecological niche which the people have carved out for themselves. Their house pattern, dress and ornaments, food and drinks, implements and domestic articles and their personal appearance speak of the climatic conditions and topography of the area.

House Type:

The Balti houses are low with flat roof and are constructed by the sun-dried bricks. Invariably, they are double storeyed *Kachcha* structures.

Plinths and foundations are raised by stones. The material of walls consists of either sunburnt bricks or stone plastered with clay. The elevation of a storey ranges between 6' or 8' due to intense cold during nights when the temperature falls as below as -17° or -23°C, and the fierce wind howl hence the height of the ceiling is kept low and the size of the windows are also kept smaller i.e. 1/2' to 5'. The roofs are flat and are supported by poplar beams of about 4"-5" in diameter, placed on opposite walls with an intervening distance of 5' to 6'. The gap between the wooden logs is covered with twigs of willow of poplar. The house tops are plastered with a thick layer of mud mixed with dry grass. Since rains are very scanty, the houses thus constructed are durable. An average dwelling measures 20'x15' and contains six rooms.

The ground floor contains four big rooms one of which is used for keeping cows and yaks (*gonval*) while the other is kept for accommodating sheep (*rogra*). A small portion of one of the corners of rogra is partitioned for the storage of the night soil which is stored from the latrine located at the first floor. Another room is used exclusively as Kitchen-cum dining room (*gosh- sakhang*) and the last room attached to *gosh* is *dewankhana* or *bokhari* and is used as a guest room. The first floor is divided into a number of rooms: one meant for storing victuals (*gran* or *zyt*), second for storing fodder (*gropyngyal* or *fungra*) and the third for storing fuel (*shilling khvang*). A small latrine is also attached with *shilling khvanq*.

The latrine (*chaksha*) is invariably located outside the house with an indigenuous device to conserve every ounce of human refuse to be used in fields as manure. This structure, though comparatively smaller in size consists of two storeys. The entrance to the laterine is through a staircase made of wood or stones. On the ground floor of *Chaksha*, a small door serves as an exit to take out the stored night soil for manuring the fields. The floor of the first storey is thatched with wooden planks. Two holes are drilled in the planks which are used as seats for defecation. The droppings get accumulated on the ground down below through these holes. In a corner of the latrinea big heap of dry dust is kept ready for sprinkling on the night soil to avoid foul odour. The dust gets mixed with the nightsoilfacilitating its extrication and sprinkling on the snow-bound field for an immature melting of ice (*sum*).

Usually there is no provision for ventilators either in the sitting rooms or in the kitchen, partly due to low ceiling and partly to check winds breaking in these rooms during winters.

The kitchen is a dinning-cum-sitting room for all seasons. Hearths, made of stone or iron and stone, occupy a central place in the kitchen and a chimney goes upto the ceiling to discharge smoke out of the kitchen. It also helps to warm the room. All members of a family huddle around the hearth on which a pot of brackish tea always keeps simmering. Only family members, friends, and relatives sit in the kitchen a little away from the ladies of the house. Dry juniper shrubs and dried cowdung are the main fuel. Those having stoves use Kerosine oil. There is normally no water out let in the kitchen. The dirty water is stored in a container and is thrown out from time to time.

Dress Pattern :

The rigours of climate in the greater Himalaya has its full reflection in the dresses of both men and women. Men wear a long woollen tunic (*guncha*) usually white, brown or black in colour. A girdle (*skarkus*) is tied around the waist. Trousers are made of wool (*dorma*) and woollen caps (*nating*) are also male apparel. The foot wear (*peposh*) are made of *pattoo* cloth and buffalo hide. The women wear black woollen tunic and trousers; a scarf (*dahun*) covers their head from an early age.

Unmarried girls wear loose white trousers whereas married ladies put on black ones. While carrying basket lodes a *sakpa* covers their back. *Sakpa* is usually made of Yak skin which keep their bodies warm specially during the winters. No shirts is put on under the tunic. Usually men and women possess a couple of sets of dresses but now mill cloth have made their way in Kargil.

A variety of items are tucked with the girdle of a man,, which consists of a pouch that contains a piece of iron and stone for making a fire (*chakmak*) a couple of small knives, a metallic or wooden box that contains tooth picks, a cup for consuming porridge or tea and while on journey a bag of parched grim flour (khachi).

The priests wear a dress which is markedly distinct from the commoners. The *aghas* wear trousers and shirt and a flowing gown (*qaba*) goes below the knee. Over *qaba* a thin black tunic (*aba*) is in variably worn. Over the head, a priest puts a round cap (*amama*). Only the accomplished priests having spent 12 to 15 years in imbibing theistic knowledge in the selected *madarasahs* of Iran and Iraq are entitled to wear this dress. A slight difference is visible in the colour of headgear don by the clergy as a symbol of their identity. The Agha or Saiyed *mujtahid* priests don a black turban whereas a non-Syed Sheikh Mujtahid dons a white. *eba, qaba* and *amama* are usually worn on in the public congregations. At home, however, the clergy wear normal dress.

Ornaments :

The Balti ornaments may be broadly divided into three categories: (i) decorative, (ii) therapeutic and (iii) sacred. Each type is described below:

Before embarking upon a description of ornaments it would be interesting to discuss yet another role played by them. It has already been stated that almost each village in Kargil has an *imambara* or *matamsara* for Moharram congregations. Men and women attend these congregations for a number of reasons (Rizvi: 1973). They implore themartyres, to help in a myriad of their problems. Womenmake an offering of their ornaments to the martyres in the Imambara known as matamsara, which becomes the property of the sacred centre. The *matamsara* management organizes periodic auctions of its movable assets. The income thus received is spent on the maintenance of the building. The prospective bidders offer a higher price than the intrinsic value of an item in order to bring merit (*sawaab*) to themselves. An ornament which is an economic asset on human body becomes a sacred relic no sooner it becomes an asset of *matamsara*. Thus the 'economic' value of such items entering from the realm of secular to sacred becomes more 'substantive' than 'formal' (Polanyi:1957). A piece of an ornament purchased from the *matamsara* is worn by women more as a sacred relic than an object of body adornment.

Decorative Ornaments:

Women, invariably decorate their body with silver ornaments from headgear to fingers. The women decorate their caps with *tumar* and the married ladies hang a pendant on both of their breasts (*pandap*). *Bramshrik*, is a pendant made of silver and is studded with semi-precious turquoise and rubies. *Nacha*, made of silver beads is used as a necklace. Another type of necklace used by the Balti women is known as *chapkali* which is also made of silver. Bangles (*Urdingu*) recent in origin, are a result of culture contact of the Kargileans with Kashmiri. They are made of glass or silver. *Phrah* is a band of *pattoo* measuring 505 mm. in breadth and 42 mm. in length studded with stones disks (*shuglo*) varying in circumference from 3 mm. to 4.50 mm.

Men do not wear any ornaments excepting finger rings made of sliver and studded with stones. Use of gold ornaments is prohibited for menby a religious fiat. Women are allowedtoweargold-jewellery but poor economy does not allow most of them to decorate their bodies with gold ornaments. However, if any one of them possesses gold ornaments she has to remove them at the time of saying *namaz* prayers.

Therapeutic Ornaments :

The people obtain charms and talismen from the Sheikh and/or Akhuns for curing various maladies. A charm, containing various verses from the holy Quran and encased in a casket made of silver (*khinchan*) is put on either around the neck or the right forearm.

Sacred Ornaments :

Ornaments purchased from *Imambara* or containing verses of Holy Quran and other charms inscribed on semi-precious stones like *naade-Ali* are worn by men and women alike partly as a mark of affiliation to their religion and partly to ward off the harmful effects of an evil eye.

Food and Drinks:

The people take their meals four times a day. The breakfast (*chinan*), usually taken around 8'O clock, consists of brackish tea (*gurgur cha*) mixed with flour of parched grim (*khachi*). The lunch (*motugizan*), taken in the afternoon, consists of leavened wheat bread, brackish tea, steamed *sattoo* seasoned with butter (*skiu*), cooked green leafy vegetables such as turnip, spinach, raddish, cabbage, *hawk* (now imported from Srinagar and available in Kargil market), onion, and cabbage seasoned with salt, chillies and tomatoas. In Wakha green peas (*shinum*) are mixed with vegetables. After lunch the people disperse for their daily chores and return around four or five O'clock in the afternoon and take refreshment (*tozar*) consisting of leavened wheat cakes, brackish tea, and boiled eggs. Dinner (*ghizbezan*), taken between eight to ten O'clock in the night, usually consists of mutton curry, vegetables, leavened wheat breads and rice (occasionally). This schedule of food consumption is uniform in Kargil but items of food vary according to varying altitudes. At higher altitudes it is not possible to raise more than one crop in a year. Green vegetables are scarce, *grim* is cultivated only when the weather permits. Green peas, wheat and barley do not sprout. People mainly depend on a single millet crop of *gangni* and *turumb*. The nature has compensated for this deficiencyby bestowing the villagers with bumperturnip crops. These gigantic tubers not only bigger in size but sweeter in taste as well. After pealing, boiling, cutting and drying, it is mixed with millet flour to prepare leavened breads. Locally available fruits like apricots, (*chuli*) and apples are consumed in plenty wherever grown in the orchards. Hardas apricots are famous for their taste and qualities.

Prohibited Items of Diet :

Crows and all birds with hooked beak are considered as the birds of prey and therefore are prohibited. Similarly, all varieties of scaleless fish are forbidden as they are believed to sustain themselves on eating flesh. Animals of prey also fall in the category of prohibited food items besides bears, mouse and hare.

Drinks :

Like other parts of western Himalayas tea (*cha*) is the main drink. A pot of water mixed with tea leaves and soda almost keeps simmering on the hearth round the clock in all seasons. Tea may be divided into two categories: *gur-gur, cha* and *lipton cha. Gur- gur cha* is prepared by putting green tea leaves in boiling water and mixing salt and soda. Soda gives the brew a pinkish hue after milk is added into it. Then, the liquid is put in a hollow container made from poplar or willow trunk and fitted with a piston like device. The brew is put in the container and a liberal amount of butter is added to it. The piston moving up and down vertically inside the container allows the butter to mix with the brew thoroughly. The vessel is known as gur-gur.

Lipton Cha, on the other hand, is alien to the customary diestary of the people. It is usually offered to the visitors and government officials etc. The people always prefer to consume brackish tea.

Qahwa is yet another popular drink offered to the distinguished guests by the aristocrate families of Kargil in dainty cups (finjaan). The brew is prepared by boiling leaves with water and seasoning it with sugar, saffron, almonds and spices. The drink is taken only on extra special occasions like the visits paid by the in-laws or political leaders etc.

Prohibited drinks :

Chang, the popular drinks of Laddakh is totally prohibited among the Balti Muslim of Kargil. They also desist from all types of wines and fermented drinks.

Narcotics

Tobacco in form of cigarettes or on a hubble-bubble is consumed by the people especially by the male members. Besides smoking there is no other form of tobacco consumption. Opium, hashish and other hard narcotics are not in use.

Food Habits and Ethnic Boundary Maintenance :

The people of Kargil largely being the Shia Ethna-e-ashari desist from accepting anything wet or cooked from a non-Muslim. There is however no restriction in accepting dry rations from non-Muslims. Many local army officers complained and felt puzzled over the behaviour of Muslim labourers of Kargil working for them as to why they do not accept cooked food and tea from the army mess even if they are hungry and tired whereas they accept dry rations gladly and cook a meal for themselves wasting their precious time and fuel. Talib, my interpretor-cum-field guide, a young boy of twelve years took his meals in Batalic Army Mess on my insistence but unfortunately he was seen by one of his co-villagers who was working there as a labourer. He was almost in tears and trembling with fear when he reported this episode to me. Lest a complaint reaches to his parents and he is punished.

The Shia Muslims of Kargil, conformed to the Islamic code of conduct as entailed in Fiqah-e-Jaffaria, are very strict in following the laid down provisions. Any deviations from these provisions is likely to incur super natural wrath (*azaab*) on them.

Weapons Implements and Domestic Articles :

The people are distinct by absence of weapons of any type. Their legends and folklores hardly suggest that they ever practiced hunting at any time excluding perhaps the days when Bonism was dominat religion of the area. Buddhism puts a stress on compassion and non violence and the same Buddhist legacy was transmitted to the people when they embraced Islam which came to Kargil more as a result of peaceful persuasion than forceful conversion. Archery, even as a Himalayan sport, does not exist among the Balti Muslims.

The agricultural implements of the people are few and simple. Plough (*hal*) are smallest in size in comparison to any other place in India. The small size of ploughs may be explained in terms of local topography. The high altitude does not allow the draught animals to pull heavy ploughs. Besides the top soil is thin and a long plough share is likely to cause more harm to soil rather than making furrows of the desired depth. A plough consists of a beam (*hales*), a yoke (*athar*), handle (*mushti*), shoe (*thoma*), and share (*pharale*). Spade (*pheonli*) consists of wooden stick (*donro*) socketed into a broad Iron shovel (*pheonli*). The implement is used as an earth mover. The Iron *phaonli* is purchased from Kargil market. Tokche is a pointed axe which is made of iron and fitted into a wooden stick (*donro*). It is usually used in kitchen gardening for making shallow holes in the ground for embedding seeds.

Household Articles :

An average Balti Muslim family in Kargil possesses a variety of utensils made of copper and aluminium, pottery of china clay, and various types of dishes and containers. Tea is served invariably in *Korol* (cup made of china clay), leavened cakes in plates of made of copper *(tabbaq)*. Some houses posses samawar (a kettle- like utensil) for preparation of *qahwa*. A *karis* made of copper or aluminium is used for storing water while taking ablutions. *Ketlis* (kettles) either made of copper or aluminium are used for pouring tea into cups while serving it to guests. *Rezm*, a wooden box is invariably kept in the kitchen which is used as a container for keeping *sattoo* flour. *Mongur* (cup) made of copper and polished from within with a coat of lead is used for serving side dishes like vegetables or meat. Mutton or vegetable curry is served by a *phogon* (spoon) made of aluminium. Brass utensils are singularly conspicuous by their absence as no significance is attached to them by the people, whereas copper utensils are commonly used as they are believed to possess some curative qualities. 'Yera' tumblers are used in almost all the houses to offer tea or water to the guests.

Interior Decoration :

The sitting arrangement is made on the floor of the room which is covered with a Kashmiri Wuggu (mat) on which a rough woollen *chari* made of coarse goat wool is spread. A carpet is laid out on the Chari. The Persian carpets are very popular which the people usually bring from the Middle East while returning from a pilgrimage. Photographs of the departed kin, cleriks, political leaders and tombs of martyres like Karbala-e-Mualla, Najaf-e- Ashraf, Samarrah, Kazmain, and Jannat-ul-Baqi adorn the walls of the Dewan-khana. Selected holy verses from Quran Sharif, and prayers like Nad-e-Ali,Aayat-ul-Kursi, the names of Panjatan-e-Pak or Chahar-da-Masoomeen also adorn the walls. The head of a household or a chief guest like Agha or Sheikh sits on the one corner of the carpet facing other audienes who sit in a parallel row in an orderly fashion. The chief guest sits on a thick cushion. There is always a provision for saying namaz prayers in the Dewan khana for the hosts as well as for guests, if any, at the appointed hour. Water for abluation *(wazu)*, and Ja-namaaz, tasbih-e-Fatima(rosary) and Sijdaqah are always kept ready with sitting room for this purpose.

Personal Appearance, Health and Hygiene:

Due to the limitations that the ecology imposes, the people can not afford to lock very cheerful rustling in silk and nylon. Scratching a livelihood from an inhospitable and rigorous climate keeps the men and women busy in all the seasons. Clothes which they wear, are rough mostly black in colour made of pattoo. Their system of values and religious sanctions too do not allow them to live a gay life: they live a simple puritanic life, working most of the times either in their fields or as labourers. A higher degree of conformity to the precepts and fundamentals of Islam has kept them away from a sheer display of wealth. The villages are beset with tuberculosis, dyspepsia, dysentry, anaemia, diarrhoea, worm and skin diseases. Low house ceilings, want of balanced food, lack of ventilation, high altitude effects, hard labour, deficient intake of milk and milk products, excessive intakes of soda bi-carbonate have made them an ideal prey of various diseases. Efforts are on the way to improve the sorry state of health of the people but a break-through is yet to be achieved. People depend on indigenous forms of medicines prescribed by the Buddhist Amchis or on therapeutic amulets prescribed by the Akhuns. Armed forces, play a significant role in improving their health conditions. An army doctor visits the villages periodically and examines all the patients at an appointed place. Though a dispensary was opened in Hardas in 1973 but no qualified doctor was posted. It was run by a compounder. There was virtually nothing in the said dispensary in the name of medicines excepting a few dozens of A.P.C. tablets.

The material culture of the Balti Muslims is the product of an ecological 'niche' that this group (carved out for itself). Its attributes differ from place to place and vary at various altitudes. Besides ecology, religion is another significant factor that effects material culture. Living in a harsh and unpredictable climate that Kargil enjoys, life is extremely precarious and difficult. An untimely gale, downpour or excesive snowfall may cause a tremendous land slide rendering cultivable lands useless for years. The vagaries of nature have made the people more god fearing with an excessive degree of conformity to the precepts of the religion that they follow. Thus their lives revolve round a number of religious performances and sacred rituals which will be described elsewhere. This also explains the presence of a matamsara and mosque in almost every village in Kargil. Thus religion is the mechanism through which people maintain a precarious balance between the nature and their material culture.

CHAPTER III

ECONOMIC STRUCTURE AND CHANGE

Traditional Economy :

The traditional economy of Laddakh was a blend of trade, pastoralism, and marginal agriculture. The green patches in the bottom of desolate mountain ranges attracted many a herders from adjoining areas to settle down in Kargil near water resources. The pastoral economy continued and still it is reflected in the cultural melieu of Kargil. Animal hides provided clothes, hair provided wool, animal refuse was dried and used as domestic fuel and milk products were the mainstay of food requirements. Barter was another important aspect of economy in Kargil. Trade links extended to Southeast Asia, Central Asia, Kashmir Valley and Himalayan Districts of Lahul, Spiti and the plains of Punjab via Zanskar. Shawl wool, borax salt, dry fruits, gold dust, eggs, and tea were the main items of export whereas finished dresses, silver, steel, shawls, butter, honey, grains and resins, torquoise and iron utensils were imported.

The traditional trade activities came to a grinding halt by early sixties of this century. Economy of the people was ruined but this vaccum was only temporary. The extension of communication network and the stationing of army near the Balti habitats created job opportunities, hence labour activities became an integral part of the economy which has been explained in terms of economic resources : land, labour and capital; economic activities pertaning to acquisition of economic resources and economic relationships that determine the economic network of the region have also been dealt here.

Economic Resources :

Economic resources are the means through which people seek their livelihood, these are closely related with the eco-system found in the region. For purposes of analysis, economic resources may be divided into land, labour, capital.

Land in Kargil :

On the basis of data gathered from the Balti villages Hardas and Wakha it is evident that each household possesses 2.42 acres of land out of which 1.63 acres is cultivable and 0.79 acres is uncultivable. Coming to per capital possession of land it was found that an individual possesses 0.29 acres of land out of which 0.25 acres of land is cultivable. In other words, 0.04 acres of land in possession of each individual is unfit for cultivation.

The following table gives distribution of land per household and per head in terms of cultivable and total landholding.

Table 1

Distribution of land per household and per capita.

Villages	Cultivable land per household (in acres)	Cultivable land per head (in acres)	Total land per house hold (in acres)	Total land per head (in acres)	No. of household	Population
Hardas	(0.97)	(0.17)	(1.80)	(0.14)	82	543
Wakha	(2.28)	(0.33)	(3.04)	(0.44)	130	893
Av.	(1.63)	(0.25)	(2.42)	(0.29)	212	1436

Hardas though nearer to the border, in smooth is topography. The village is settled in a form of a longitudinal strip on the banks of Dras river. The danger of land slides and floods during summers when streams touch a high level due to melting of snow have effected little the size of cultivable land. Here the size of landholding possessed by a household and an individual is 1.60 acres and 0.14 acres respectively, of which cultivable land per household is 0.97 acres and per individual is 0.17 acres.

In Wakha, the size of landholding possessed by both a household (3.04 acres) and an individual (0.44 acres) is abnormally high. This anamoly may be explained in terms of topography, ethnic composition and distant situation of the village from borders. Wakha is settled in a broad valley hence more land is available for cultivation. It is predominantly inhabited by 530 Buddhists and 363 Muslims. Buddhists are polyandrous and polyandry helps to maintain the size of a land holdingsandserves as an impediment to fragmentationof land whereas Muslims being usually monogamous possess small sized landholdings due to fragmentation of land with increasing size of their population. The size of landholding possessed by the Muslims of Wakha, however, shows thattheyhave got an edge in this respectovertheir brotheren in Hardas. The following table brings the above point at home.

Table. 2

Distribution of land possessed by Muslims.

Village	Size of cultivable land per household	Size of cultivable land per head	Total land per house	Total land per capita	No. of house hold	Population (Muslim)	Total Populaiton
Hardas	1.93	0.33	2.16	0.28	81	543	543
Wakha	3.16	0.56	4.54	0.83	64	363	893

The above table shows that each Muslim household in Wakha possesses 4.54 acres out of which 3.16 acres of land is cultivable. On the other hand, looking at per capita size of landholding a Muslim of Wakha possesses 0.83 acres of land out of which 8.56 acres is cultivable. In Hardas each Muslim household possesses 2.16 acres of land out of which 1.93 acres is cultivable and the remaining 0.23 acres is not fit for cultivation.

Distribution of Households According to Size of Landholdings :

In Hardas the size of landholdings is smaller in comparison to Wakha. In Hardas 96.34 per cent households possess landholdings whose size vary between 0.25 to 4.00 acres, and only one household possessed land between 4.00 to 8.00 acres. In Wakha however, bigger size of land holdings to the tone of 2 to 8 acres are possessed by 73.07 percent households. This is followed by 5.39 per cent households possessing land between 8.00 to 12.00 acres, 2.31 percent households between 12.00 to 16.00 acres, 0.77 percent each between 16.00 to 20.00 acres and 20.00 to 24.00 acres. Thus, it is seen that the size of the landholdings in Wakha is larger as when compared to that in Hardas. The further details may be seen from the table below. In other words altitude seems to be inversely related with the size of landholding.

Table. 3

Distribution of households according to size of landholdings.

Size of cultivable land holdings in acres	Hardas No. of house hold	%	Wakha No. of house hold	%
No. land	2	2.44	2	1.54
less then 0.25	-	-	-	-
0.25 + 2.00	38	46.34	21	16.15
2.00 + 4.00	41	50.00	48	36.92 } 73.0'
4.00 + 8.00	1	1.22	47	36.15
8.00 + 12.00	-	-	7	5.39
12.00 + 16.00	-	-	3	2.31
16.00 + 20.00	-	-	1	0.77
20.00 + 24.00	-	-	1	0.77
Total :	82	100.00	130	100.00

Thus the above table shows that the size of land holding in Hardas mainly vary between 0.25 acres to 4.00 acres whereas in Wakha they mainly vary between 0.25 acres to 16.00 acres and also two households possess land between 16.00 acres to 24.00 acres. Thus, we see an increase in the size of the landholding from Hardas to Wakha. This may be attributed to the reason that the altitude seems to be inversely related to the size of the land holding. Bigger size of landholding in Wakha, as said earlier, is also due to its predominant Buddhist population and greater availability of land. There are 2 landless families each in Hardas and Wakha.

Types of land :

There are five following types of land in Kargil.

(a) **Muljing :** *Muljing* is the best type of land situated near the source of irrigation. Whenever possible two crops may be obtained. The rate of revenue for muljing is Rs. 4/- per acre.

(b) **Burjing :** Burjing gives a single crop in a year because of its inferior quality but it is closer to the sources of irrigation.

(c) **Chas-saagzar :** *Chas-saagzar* is attached with a homestead for purposes of kitchen gardening. The rate of revenue is Rs. 4/- per acre.

(d) **Tha-jing :** *Tha* (away) *Jing* is the land situated away from the village on the high hills or near the flowing rivers. The rate of revenue for *tha-Jing* is Rs. 3/- per acre.

(e) **01 :** 01 is grass land where fodder, grass or bushes are harvested and stored for winter as fodder for animals and fuels for domestic consumption.

Ravenue Collection :

During the regime of Dogra rulers (*shakhsi-raaj*), the responsibility of revenue collection was entirely of village *numbardar*, who used to get a commission equivalent to 2C.00 per cent of the total revenue received from a village (*panjotra*). After annexation of Kargil with Jammu and Kashmir State, the land owners paying revenue upto a sum of Rs 9.00 or less were exempted from payment of revenue to the government. This brought about a change in the role of village *numbardar* as collector of revenue. This aspect of change will be dealt in later.

Pattern of Ownership :

The pattern of land ownership is collective and lineage based. A lineage, in return, allocates parcels of land among its various member households. In case, a person dies without leaving a patential heir, the land of the deceased goes to the lineage and is shared equally by all member households of lineage. If the size of the land holding of the deceased is too small to be divided, it is sold out and the sum thus received is equally divided among member households.

Inheritance :

Land is inherited by both male and female issues according to the provisions of *shara*. The male issue of a deceased are entitled for two third portion of the land where as female issues receive one third portion of the land left behind by the deceased. A girl of deceased does not usually claim her portion of landed property as her maintenance and marriage is the responsibility of her brothers, but if she claims she can receive it. No cases of such claims were reported from Kargil.

AGRICULTURE

Agriculture in Kargil as a whole occupies 41.90 per cent land and total non-cultivable land is 58.10 per cent (Census of India - 1961). Data collected from two Balti villages, however show a higher percentage of cultivable land (68.22) and a lower percentage of non-cultivable land (31.78). The village wise distribution of cultivable and non-cultivable land is given in the following table.

Table. 4

Village -wise distribution of cultivable and non-cultivable land in Kargil.

Villages	Total land (in acres)	Cultivable land (in acres)	Percentage land	Non-cultivable (in acres)	Percentage
Hardas	87.50	48.87	55.86	38.62	44.14
Wakha	345.50	246.50	71.35	99.00	28.65
Total	433.00	295.37	68.22	137.62	31.78

It is clear from the above table that Hardas, though situated at relatively lower altitude but nearer to the border shows slightly smaller size of non-cultivable land (44.14 per cent) and higher size of cultivable land (55.86 percent). Contrary to Hardas, Wakha shows larger size of cultivable land which stands 71.35 per cent and the smaller size of non-cultivable land (28.65 per cent). Thus the trend that is descernible from the above table is that the size of cultivable land shrinks with the increase in the altitudinal height. Correspondingly higher is the altitude bigger is the size of non-cultivable land. The factors responsible are both climatic and man-made. An intensive network of subterrainean mines has also helped in increasing the size of non-cultivable land in the border villages.

Crops :

Villages with a moderate climate produce two crops : the first crop is known as *thoq* and the second *chyut*. The lands remain fallow under a thick blanket of snow from December to March. Agricultural operations begin with Navroz (the Persian New Year's Day) which falls on March 21 but related agricultural activities start much earlier. The agricultural activities will be described later. The main crops consist of millets, barley and turnip in high altitude villages whereas villages situated in lower altitudes (9,000 ft to 11,000 ft) beside-barley (yo),grow wheat (*kanak/tro*), grim (*nas*) and peas (*shanma*) also.

Water Management :

Agricultural production in Kargil entirely depends on irrigation. Since the area is out of monsoon zone, the water management in Kargil is entirely different from monsoon prone areas. Shortage of irrigation water leads to low agriculatural output. Rivers or streams flow beside most of the villages in Kargil but their water remain untapped due to absence of lift irrigation devices.

Water for drinking and irrigation is brought in canals or aqueducts (*kuhls*). The *kuhls* originate from upstream of a river and pass sevaral hundred feet above surface of a village. Each hamlet in a village has a pond to store water for *kuhls* for irrigation and cleaning clothes and utensils. Animals also drink water from these ponds. The maintenance of *kuhl* is the collective responsibility of villagers as frequent landslides stiffle the flow of water in the canal. When water flow stops, the numbardar of the villagepicks up a few people and instructs them to inspect the *kuhl* and repair the damage done to it, if any.

There is a regular time table for use of water in Hardas that allocates water in such a manner that each lineage gets its share of water after 9 days. The following table shows various lineages with respective numbers of member households and duration of time allotted to each lineage.

Table. 5

Time Schedule for irrigation from Kuhl Wath in Hardas.

Sl.No.	Name of lineage	No. of house holds	Time allotted for irrigation (in hrs.)	Remarks
1.	Rulba-pa	9	36	
2.	Hussain Meripa	9	15	
3.	Majan-pa	8	9	
4.	Skitali-pa	7	15	
5.	Haider-pa	7	6	
6.	Ashur-pa	6	12	
7.	Khache-pa	6	6	
8.	Kalbi-pa	5	24	
9.	Ghote-pa	3	12	
10.	Dolthoq-pa	3	6	
11.	Mala-pa	3	12	
12.	Syed-pa	3	12	
13.	Arab-pa	2	6	
14.	Rahman-pa	2	9	
15.	Shafi-pa	2	-	Later immigrants.
16.	Beumo-pa	1	6	
17.	Barvesh-pa	1	6	
18.	Goya-pa	1	12	
19.	Karpochuli-pa	1	6	
20.	Kharma-pa	1	-	-do-
21.	Purig-pa	1	6	
		81	216	

AGRICULTURAL PRODUCTION :

The unit for agricultural production in Kargil is Khal which is equal to 15 kilogrammes. Data collected from the two villages show a varying picture of food production in Kargil. The figures are furnished in the following table.

Table. 6

Food production.

Villages	Total production (in Kgs)	Production per house hold (in kgs)	Production per capita (in kgs)	Production per acre of cultivable land (in kgs)
Hardas	30300	369.5	55.8	310.0
Wakha	107910	830.1	120.8	182.0

The Border village Hardas shows an yield of 310.10 kgs/acre whereas Wakha shows a lower yeild of 182.00 kgs per acre of cultivable land. In total production per capita Wakha is ahead of Hardas with an yeild of 55.8 kgs per head. Similar picture emerges from the figures of production per household and the total production in a year. In addition to food grains Hardas produces 2991 kgs of dry apricots. On average a single household produces 36.5 kgs of dry apricots and sells it in Kargil market. The selling price of dry apricots in Kargil market at the time of investigation was Rs. 8/-per kg.

Labour :

Labour is another important economic resource which helps the people to compensate the shortfall in an agricultural produces. For purposes of analysis the labour force in Kargil has been divided into two broad categories which are stated below :

(i) Auxilary labour force and :

(ii) Effective labour force :

(i) Auxilary Labour Force :

The members of auxiliary labour force depend on effective labour force for their subsistence. It does not imply, however, that the members of auxiliary labour force do not contribute to the economy of the groups or their role is insignificant in the process of capital formation. Children from very early age make their contribution to household economy according to their mite. Similarly older people too contribute to the household economy by assuming a supervisory role in day to day economic activities of the hoseholds. However, their full participation in the economy can be easily ruled out because the factor of age. Members of this group belong to the age category of below fourteen years and above sixty years.

(ii) Effective Labour Force :

The age group of effective labour force ranges from above 14 years to 60 years as the people belonging to these age groups are major bread earners for their households. Table No 7 given below gives distribution of the types of labour force into auxiliary and effective labour. @PARA MORE = In the villages under study 38.58 per cent population belongs to the age group of 0 to 14 years and 6.82 per cent belongs tothe people whose age is above 60 years. Thus 45.40 percent population belongs to the age group of 0 to 14 years or above. The percentage of the population in the age group of 14 to 34 years is 32.66 per cent and between 34 to 60 years is 21.94 per cent. Thus the effective labour force constitutes 54.60 per cent of the totalpopulation whereas the auxiliary labour force works out to 45.40 per cent of the total population.

Looking at the village wise labour force it was found that Wakha has an auxiliary labour force of 42.55 per cent whereas Hardas shows higher percentage of auxiliary labour force which stands at 50.09 per cent. But coming to the effective labour force it was found that it is lower in case of Hardas with 49.91 per cent, whereas Wakha shows a higher effective labour force of 57.45 per cent. Hardas (49.91) and Wakha (57.45) are no where nearer to over all percentage. Another way of looking at labour as an economic resource is to divide it to self-employed labour force and employed labour force.

The self-employed labour force consist of those individuals who indulge in labour activities for themselves and, thus, they do not draw any emoluments in return of their services. This includes women, children and men who work for themselves. Self-employed labour activities may be extended to collective Kinship-based tasks, viz., maintenance of *kuhl* mosques and *matamsara*. Members of a lineage help each other in house building activities. Masons, carpenters and ironsmiths of a single lineage contribute their labour without charging any fee. The employed labour force consist of those individuals who receive remunerations from an employer who may or may not belong to the same group to which a wage earner belongs

Table 7

Disribution of population into age groups composing auxiliary and effective labour force.

Village	HARDAS				WAKHA				GRAND TOTAL			
	Male	Female	Total	Percentage	Male	Female	Total	Percentage	Male	Female	Total	Percentage
0-14	133	102	235	43.28	163	156	319	35.72	296	258	554	38.58
14+-34	84	76	162	29.84	156	151	307	34.38	240	229	469	32.66
34+-60	57	52	109	20.07	118	88	206	23.07	175	140	315	21.94
60+ and above	21	16	37	6.81	32	29	61	6.83	53	45	98	6.82
Total	295	248	543	100.00	469	424	893	100.00	764	672	1436	100.00
Auxiliary labour force	154	118	272	50.09	195	185	380	42.55	349	303	652	45.40
Effective labour force	141	130	271	49.91	274	239	513	57.45	415	369	784	54.60
E-IL	295	248	543	100.00	469	424	893	100.00	764	672	1436	100.00

The following table shows the number of effective labour force in the two villages under study and the number of employed persons working for others and receiving remunerations in return to their services.

Table. 8

Village wise distribution of employed persons from effective from effective labour force.

Village	No. of effective labour force	No. of employed	Percentage
Hardas	271	57	21.03
Wakha	513	101	19.69
Total :	784	158	20.15

The extent of employment in the two villages of Kargil is 20.15 per cent. In Hardas 21.03 per cent are employed whereas the extent of employment is less in Wakha which stand at 19.69 per cent of the total number of effective labour force.

Capital :

"Capital" represents a stock of goods and services not devoted to immediate consumption but operated to increase the value of consumption in future periods either directly or indirectly through production" (Firth and Yamey : 1969). The deficient agricultural production hardly help the process of capital formation in Kargil even in meeting the basic requirements of the populaiton. Ornaments bear more social and ritual value than as an item of capital. Animal wealth, however, may be considered as a real item of capital.

The distribution of animal wealth in the two villages of Kargil under study is given in the table no 9.

The over all man animal ratio in the two villages of Kargil stands at 1:1.52 and over all household animal ratio is 1:10.26. Like all other economic resources Hardas is deficient in animal wealth too. Man-animal ratio of Hardas is 1:07 and household-animal ratio is 1:47. Wakha is far ahead than Hardas so far as the two ratios are concerned. The village shows 1:2.1 and 1:14.6 man-animal and household ratios respectively.

Table 9

Distribution of animal wealth man-animal and household -animal ratio.

Villages	Horpe	Cow	Bullock	Zho/Zhom	Goat	Sheep	Total	Man-animal ratio	Man-house hold ratio	Population	No. of household
Hardas	28.72	nil	nil	71	172	113	384	1:0.7	1:4.7	543	82
Percentage	27.72			27.31	18.22	15.50	17.65				
Wakha	73	126	16	189	772	616	1792	1:2.1	1:14.6	893	130
Percentage	72.28	100.00	100.00	72.69	81.78	84.50	82.35				
Total	101	126	16	260	944	729	2176	1:1.52	1:10.26	1436	212
	100.00	100.00	100.00	100.00	100.00	100.00	100.00				

It is also evident that the mum species of cattle are Zho/zhomo (a mixed breed of Yak and cow) bullock and horses/ponies. Each species of animal has a vital economic role to perform. It is therefore, worthwhile to judge the merit of each animal in over all economy of the people in the paragraphs to follow:

Horses/Ponies :

Horses and ponies have been enumerated together as their economic value as a beast of burden is similar. Wakha has more horses than Hardas. A horse is a sign of social prestige of its owner. It not only plays an important role as a means of transportation but also satisfies the recreational needs of the people in general and of Buddhits in particular. Buddhists are extremely fond of horse- polo(*chaugan*). A swift footed and steady horse is better suited to the winners of the game than the slow ponies. Ponies play a vital role in the process of capital formation especially in border villages. A head of pony earns as much as Rs. 800/- per month for its owner asit is detailed for transporting supplies to the places those which are still not connected by roads. There are 28 ponies in Hardas and 73 in Wakha. In terms of percentage, the entire animal wealth, Hardas possess 27.72 per cent ponies and Wakha 72.28 per cent. Low percentage of horses in Hardas is mainly due to lack of grazing in the vicinity of the village. Many ponies have lost their lives by hitting mines which were extensively laid during the past.

Cows :

Cows were found only in Wakha. Hardas draws a blank so far as cows are concerned. Absence of cows has resulted in shortage of milk in the village and the villagers are forced to whiten their tea cups with a thick paste of apricot seads. 16 bullocks were found in Wakha whereas none were found in Hardas.

Zho/Zhomo :

Zho is the mixed breed of Yak and cow. The female is known as *Zhomo* which is reared with a view to augment milk supply. Large *zhos* are 6 feet, high at shoulder humps but the *zhomo* are much smaller. The hair is black and short except on the flank and tail where it forms a long shaggy fringe. *Zho* or *zhomos* are not only used as beasts of burden but also yoked in ploughs. The utility of the animals speaks itself when its distribution in the villages is taken into consideration. There ae 71 zhos in Hardas and 189 in Wakha.

Due to scarcity of water and pastureage coupled with hazards of mine explosion, the *zhomos* are sent away to Dras or Kartse from the border village of Hardas from April to November every year.

Goats :

Goats outnumber all other species of animals enumerated from the two villages. Out of the 944 goats enumerated in the two villages 172 (18.22 per cent) were found in Hardas and 772 (81.78 per cent) in Wakha.

Goats in Kargil are raised as a main source of milk and mutton supply. Minimisation of herds is essential not only to augment the source of food supply but also due to non-availability of fodder during prolonged arctic winters. Each Muslim household in Kargil sacrifices a goat on special occasions like Moharram, Id- e-qurban, Strupla and Losar. On Losar (Buddhist New Year) a number of goats is slaughtered and kept for future consumption during winters when availability of food articles is almost nil. All streams freeze, and the narrow brittle tracks remain snowlocked resulting into a complete disruption of movement from one house to another in the same village. Besides a thick hair which is spun into long strips which after sewn together make a mattress (*Chari*). Goat dung is a good fuel especially during winters, and an ideal manure for kitchen gardens.

Sheep :

The number of sheep reared in the two villages was found smaller than goats. There are 729 sheep in all, out of which 113 (15.50 per cent) were found in Hardas and 616 (84.50 per cent) in Wakha. The main reason for smaller number of sheep may be attributed to inferiority and hardness of its mutton that requires more fuel forcooking. However, wool and milk compensate for the inferior quality of sheep mutton. The wool extracted from sheep is first carded and then spun on wooden spindles into long threads from which balls are made in different sizes. Now the spun wool is used for weaving long and broad strips of *potttoo* from which long coats, caps, coarse shawls and footwear are made. Like goats sheep too are sacrificed on the occasions mentioned above.

Taking all species of animals into account Hardas shares 17.65 per cent of animal wealth and Wakha 82.35 per cent. The reasons for lower possession of animal wealth in the border village of Hardas may again be all attributed to "borderness" more than the altitudinal variations.

Poultry :

Poultry is mainly raised for self consumption and the fowl birds are hardly sold out for cash. The Buddhists of Wakha, however, were seen sitting on the roadside and selling the eggs and fowl birds to the passing military conveys. The price of egg was recorded as 0.50 paise a piece and a fowl Rs. 40.00 per bead of bird at the time of field investigation.

Economic Resources in Nutshell :

Taking all three economic parameters viz., land, labour and capital into consideration, it was found, that Hardas occupies a lower place in the ladder of economic resource when compared to that of Wakha. Factors responisble for disparity in economic resources in these two study-villages have already been described but it will be worth while once more to give a brief enumeration of those factors which may be termed as i) borderness, ii) ecological setting of village and iii) the changes experienced by the inhabitants of the two villages since 1947.

(i) Borderness:

Situated near the line of actual control, Hardas has experiencedthree successivewarsin1947,1965 and 1971. Consequently, vast tracts of cultivable land with excellent irrigational facilities came under enemy's occupation and were heavily mined. The people of Hardas were not only deprived of their wet cultivable lands but had to suffer heavy losses in animal wealth due to triggering of mine explosions. The size of herds shrank considerably as grazing grounds for animals were also declared unsafe for grazing. Due to shortage of fodder, animals rush towards green patches of land for grazing and if not checked in time get themselves killed. Ponies and horses run helter and skelter making it difficult for the owners to stop them from entering into 'death zone'. Hence, a shrunk size of cultivable land and depleting animal population casts its reflection on the over all economy of the people. Wakha, on the other hand, has never faced the problem of 'borderness' as it is situated far away from the line of actual control. Wakha river flows right in the middle of the village at an even surface level. Hence, irrigation is not as big a problem as it is in the Kuhl-fed village of Hardas. Enough land is available at Wakha as mountain ranges do not run parallelly and close to each other as in case of Hardas.

Having discussed the existing economic resources found in Hardas and Wakha, it will be appropriate to describe as how these resources are procured, and utilised. Hence, activities pertaining to food-gathering, agriculatural and horticulture will be described in details. Activities pertaining to labour as a secondary occupation will also be brought to relief. Raising of animal herds is an important economic activity next to agriculture. This will also be discussed briefly. Dependence of man on the super-natural forces is greater in extreme climates. Hence, the performance of certain rituals for augmentation of economic resource, may also be termed as an important socio-economic activity. Thus, a description of a few activities connected with the efforts to procure better economic resources, will not be out of place.

ECONOMIC ACTIVITIES

Gathering Activities :

There is not much to collect from the denuded mountains of Kargil except small juniper bushes, which, growing spontaneously provides a good fuel for winter to keep the bodies and hearths warm. During summers small boys, girls and housewives walk 5 to 10 kms every day with their conical wicker baskets tucking on their back to fetch the wildly grown bush and the droppings of animals. In the evening the baskets are unloaded on the flat roof-tops for drying up. Later, they are stacked neatly. Collection of fuel is mainly the women's domain. Once Kargil might have been a good hunting ground with ibex, wild sheep and goats but now people have almost forgotten the art of hunting that is still prevalent in the neighbouring Zanskar and Spiti valleys. Hunting has become a part of Balti folklore.

Agricultural Activities :

All agricultural activities remain paralysed from the middle of November to the middle of March as the fields remain snow-bound during the prolonged arctic winter. Feeble March sun rays hardly penetrate the thick blanket of snow covering the fields. Hence people have evolved a technique for premature melting of snow through artificial device which is known as *sa* which implies that every ounce of humane refuse ought to be preserved in family latrines (*chaksa*) to be used as manure. The enriched dust is removed from latrines and sprinkled on the surface of ice after Navroz falling on March 21. The dark soil concentrates the sun's rays and causes snow to melt quickly. Thus, the fields are free from snow and ready for cultivation.

Ploughing :

Ploughing (*jin changet*) is done by men in April with the help of a small plough yoked with bullocks or zombas.

Sowing :

Both men and women participate in sowing (*shalba*) by broadcasting method in the months of July and August.

Irrigation :

The main source of irrigation (*jinchotang*) is artificial aqueducts (*kuhl*). When water is released from a *kuhl* for the family of a particular lineage, all its member households send their male and female members for making channels, damming and preparation of beds in the field.

Weeding :

Weeding (*yurma*) is done by both men and women. A field undergoes this operation thrice in the duration of a crop.

Harvesting :

Harvesting (*schumet*) is done in the month of September in which women participate actively. Sickles are not used for harvesting lest the brittle dry shears disintegrate due to impact of a sickle. The stalks are left in the field to dry due to brief summer in which barley does not get sufficient time to ripen. After harvestingwomenclear a patch of land to be usedasgranary (*Khiuskoret*). Winnowing (*asoumeti*) is done by lifting hay by an iron shoval upto one's head level and dropping the contents on the ground. The wind separates hay from food-grains. The good foodgrains are stored in goat-skin bags (*Kelbur*).

Processing :

The barley is first washed (*tso-Ka Khvut*) and left in open to get dried. Another method is to sprinkle water on the gunny bag in which barley is stored allowing the grains to germinate and then the grains are spread in open vessels by heating it with sand (*changhi Khayus schewet*). The roasted barley is now taken to water-mill for grinding (*ranthog taget*). The barley flour (*tsampa*) is the staple diet of the villagers about which a reference has already been made. "The Himalayan diet of *tsampa* further makes travelling simple as this cooked flour is eaten cold and keeps for a long time. A small bag of *tsampa* can see a traveller on his way for weeks" (Peissel : 1979).

Kitchen Gardening :

Every house has a small kitchen garden which is known as *chas* or *sas* or *sagzar* in which onions, turnips, (*mulaq*), potatoes (*aloo*), radish (*durpo*), cabbage (*gobhi*), spinach (*hanti*) and peas (*shanma*) are grown. Sowing, manuring, irrigation, harvesting and drying of *sas* products are mainly women's job. Green sprouts of spinach, cabbage, and turnip are plucked and woven into ropes which are dried in sun light for future consumption during winters when vegetabels can neither be grown nor obtained by any other source. The tubers of turnip, onions and potatoes are left under ground where not only they grow in size but can be preserved for longer period of time. When all dried leafy vegetable are exhausted in winters, the tubers are dug out as per requirement of a family.

Horticulture :

Apricots, mulberries, apples and grapes are the fruits grown in the orchards of Kargil. Hardas is famous for its apricots (*chuli*) which is a blend of golden and vermillion in colour when fully ripened. The other variety is green with a splash of maroon tinge and is widely, known as *Karpo-chuli* (Kar/white; chuli/apricots). The latter variety was noticed at Garkoon only. The ripened apricots are spread on huge boulders for drying. Apples and mulberries are usually meant for self consumption unlike grapes and apricots which are good cash crops. The seeds of apricot are also collected and stored. Its Kernal is highly valued for its oil and various other curative properties. When milk is scarce during summers as animals are driven for grazing in the far flung Dras Valley a thick paste of apricot seeds is used for whitening tea.

ECONOMIC RELATIONSHIPS

Economic relationships among the various segments of a society or between various societies are mainly determined by the availability of economic resources and their proper utilisation. The very basic human tendency of various individuals or groups to monopolise and exploit economic resources for their own benefit at the cost of others lead to deterioration and set back in these ties. A picture of worsening economic relationships in Hardas has been portryed below to bring the point at home. At the time of investigation the village population in Hardas was polarised into two factions say faction - 1(f.1) and faction-2(f.2)-The population of f.1 is 15.65 per cent of the total village population but owns 31.02 per cent of total cultivable land in the village; the percentage of their agricultural products is 31.88. They consume 29.17 per cent of available water resources and possess 32.73 per cent of the total animal wealth.

Hence the ratio between their population and all economic resources was found approximately to be 1:2 whereas the economic resources and population ratio in f.2 was 1:1. This inequitable distribution of economic resources was a major factor of group conflict in Hardas which manifested itself into brawls, altercations, throwing of allegations and counter-allegation and deterioration of social relationship between the two factions of the village. All efforts to resolve this conflict have failed to make any headway.

At inter-village level Karkit and Hardas were engaged in a dispute on a *Kuhl* which was carved out from *Karkit nalah* near Majdas, a hamlet of Karkit. It was alleged that the members of f.1 incited the villagers of Karkit from whose lands the proposed *Kuhl* was to pass that their lands were in danger and may be taken by some villagers of Hardas (the members of faction f.2 were facing acute scarcity of water and they took an initiative to construct another *Kuhl*) without any compensation. The matter was under litigation.

Army employs at least one member from each household of the village from border villages. The relationship between the employers and employees is pleasant. The villagers who remained under alien forces for few months and suffered with the consequences of three successive wars have developed a sense of admiration for valour and high standards of discipline shown by Indian Army. Welfare activities started by army officers and their wives have brought the former closer to the people's heart. An army doctor visits all border villages periodically and distributes medicines. Army officers, on their routine visits to the border villages, exhort the villagers to send their children to schools and enhance standards of cleanliness and personal hygiene. Hence Indian Army are not only doing the job of protecting the people's health and economy but are also acting as an effective agent of social change. However, it is highly desirable that if the members of armed forces could be more closely acquainted with the traditions and customary practices of the villagers.

The communication gap between the armed forces and the local Balti has given rise to some avoidable misunderstandings. Some army officers complained that inspite of their best efforts, they have not been able to win the confidence of the people. They also alleged that the locals refuse to accept cooked food from the former, instead the latter prepare their own tea from sugar and tea leaves given by army. This attitude baffles the minds of officers which they attribute to indifferent attitude of the people towards army. The villagers on the other hand, who belong to the Shia fact of Islam, feel that their code of conduct prohibits them to eat anything wet which is being touched by a non-Muslim. Here the concept of taboo is more at work than the concept of pollution that determines the status and social position of a group in a hierarchical arrangement of various status oriented groups. This shows the people's higher sense of alienation from the army whom the people otherwise consider as their protectors.

CHAPTER IV

SOCIAL STRUCTURE AND CHANGE

The Balti living in Kargil are scattered from Skardo to Kargil and further east of Leh where there is village named Chushot consisting of well above hundred families. Purgis too claim themselves to be Baltis but Baltis refer to the former by the term Purig-pa, i.e., the people of Purik. The term Purgi, or Purki seems to be derived from the term Purik-pa. Hardas is a village where 74 Balti families were residing besides 6 Khachapa (Kashmiris)

and one Purig-pa families. The six Kashmiri families trace their descent from a Kashmiri soldier who was in the service of Zorawar Singh. A war between Zorwar Singh and Laddakhi Kings ensued near Zojila in which Zorawar Singh with his forces perished. One of his soldiers took shelter in Hardas village while being hotly chased by the victorious armies. The villagers of Hardas, mostly Baltis, allowed him to settle down in the village. The said Kashmiri soldier, who was a Sunni by faith was later converted to Shiism and his descendants now constitute of six families in the village. Another non-Balti family is of Purig-pa, a *makpa*, who married with a Balti lady of the village and settled down in the village permanently.

By virtue of their social status the population of Hardas may be put in the following hierarchical order.

Agha — Syed clergy (*mujtahid*)
(Trained abroad)

Shaikh — Non-Syed clergy (*mujtahid*)
(Trained abroad)

Akhun — Indigenous clergy
(Trained in India)

Haji — Pilgrims who have returned from the pilgrim of Iraq and Iran.

Saget — Farmers.

Agha :

The term Agha is the derivation of the Persian term *a:qa* meaning 'master', a title exclusively reserved for Syeids who are the descendant of the Prophet Mohammad (S.A) through his daughter Fatima (S.A.). The consanguinous proximity of the Agha with the Prophet Mohammad (S.A.) gives them a higher pedastal in the overall social hierarchy of the region. In Kargil, the most reverant are the Agha *mujtahids* who complete a long stint of theistic learning in the Islamic *madarasahs* situated in Iraq and Iran. Hardas has none of Agha *mujtahids*. However, among the non-mujtahid Aghas of Hardas two families of Saiyids were invited from Kharmang by the villagers of Hardas to stay amongst them to guide the people towards the path of righteousness. These families are known as Saiyid-pa. None of them own any cultivable land nor they involve themselves actively in ordinary economic activities. Their time is mostly devoted in imparting theological learning to the young boys. Their sole means of livelihood is *male-saadaat* portion of the *Khums* levy which every Shia individual has to pay at the rate of 1/5th of the total annual savings at the end of each year. The *Khums* levy is divided into two parts : a) *mal-e- saadat* and b) *mal-e-Imam. Male-Saadat* is again divided into two equal parts, one part goes to Seiyids and the other part is donated for the maintenance of Islamic Madarasahs in India or abroad. Similarly the mal-e-Imam portion of the Khumas levy is also divided into two equal parts, one part is spent on orphans, widows and other deserving people and half of it gocs to the mujtahids who are the deputies of the *Imam-a-waqt* (the contemporary living 12th Imam-al-Mahdi, A.S.). Agha Haider came from Karmang 50 years ago on the invitation of the villagers of Hardas and married with a lady of Dolthoqpa lineage. His elder son Mehdi Shah married in Mala-pa lineage.

Sheikh :

The Sheikhs are autochthonous *mujtahid* priests by virtue of their theistic accomplishment in the *madarsahs* situated in Iraq and Persia. Unlike Aghas, Sheikhs take interest day to day socio-economic activities of not only the village but in their respective families too. Sheikh Hasan of Hardas was seen carrying his agricultural and horticultural produces to Kargil market for sale. He, with the help of other members of his family, was seen briskly involved in the construction of his house. During the summers he goes to Srinagar for purchasing tea leaves, salt and butter for winters. The status of the Sheikhs is an achieved status as he may belong to any stratum of the society. He becomes a high priest by virtue of his inclination, means and labour. Sheikh Moosa of Wakha and Sheikh Mohd. Ali of Karkit were less fortunate in this respect. Sheikh Moosa, apparently suffering with spondilitis went to Iraq for seeking the degree of *ijtihaad* but had to return without completing his education as he fell sick at Iraq. Sheikh Mohammad Ali of Karkit returned from Iraq as a *mujtahid* but suffered with a stroke of paralysis and was admitted to a hospital at Srinagar. After three months of hospitalistion he returned to Karkit amidst great rejoicing. How Sheikhs are treated by villager became apparent on July 4, 1973, the day Sheikh Ali was to return to Karkit after his prolonged treatment. All male members of the village went to Dras to receive him. A pony was also taken to Dras for bringing him back to the village. The villagers awaited the arrival of Sheikh but he did not turn up because on the day he was to arrive at Dras he could not be discharged from the hospital. The villagers returned well after the dusk rather disappointed. The next evening the news reached Karkit that Sheikh Ali has reached at the Base at 'K' bridge. All villagers ran towards the 'k' bridge. The Sheikh arrived on a pony around nine o'clock in the night. All villagers went to pay respect to the Sheikh and his room remained over- crowded with the visitors till late in the night. The next day a ram was slaughtered by the villagers as an offering to Imam by whose blessings Sheikh Ali could regain his health (though partially). A feast was arranged in the afternoon in which one member from the each family of the village participated besides all male members of Sheikhs own *gatti.*

Akhun :

The Akhun, too belong to the class of clergy but they occupy a relatively lower place in the priestly class as his theological training terminates in the local *madarsaha* only. However, the Akhun specialises in giving charms, talisman and amulets to ward off an evil spirit causing various diseases. He also supervises all the life cycle rituals in the village. A profound knowledge of herbaria helps him to cure patients with *dawa* and *dua* (medicines and prayers). In short he is almost a counterpart of the Buddhists' *amchi.* Akhun is a wordly man in real sense of the term. The Akhun of Hardaswas servingasthevillagebranchpostmaster. Similarly, Akhun Taqi of Wakha was the Naib Sarpanch of the statutory village panchayat.

Haji :

Haji is a commoner with a difference . In Kargil this epithet is bestowed on those who return after visiting the tombs of Imams and *ahle-bait* situated in Iraq, Iran and Syria. In the common parlance a Haji is one who returns after performance of Haj pilgrim at Kaaba situated in the city of Mecca (Saudi Arabia). None of the Hajis, in Hardas however, ever visited Macca but had been to various pilgrim centres of Iraq and Iran. The Hajis enjoy a relatively higher soical prestige vis-a-vis a farmer (*saget*) in the village. They usually belong to economiclly well off section of the village population as a considerable expenditure is involved in making the pilgrimage. A common villager saves throughout his life with a burning ambition to pay a visit to at least once in his life time to the sacred graves of the Imams and the Prophet Mohammad (S.A.). The participation of a Haji in the spheres of the sacred as well as the secular activities of the family, lineage or the village is in no way different from an ordinary *saget* who are the tillers of the soil, the ordinary farmers and labourers. Specialisation in certain occupations, which are named below, gives rise to various classes of artisans. The following table furnishes a list of artisan groups among the Baltis of Hardas.

Table. 10

Artisan groups among the Baltis of Hardas.

Sl. No	Name of occupation	English equivalent	Pursued by	Lineage	Remark
1.	Garba	Iron Smith	Hussain	Ghote'-pa	
			Ali	Skit Ali-pa	
2.	Lamkhan	Cobblar	Haji Ibrahim	Ghote'-pa	
			Haji Haider	Rulba-pa	
3.	Shinkhan	Carpenter	Ghulam	Ashur-pa	
			Ghulam Ali	Khache'-pa	
			Hasan S/O Raza	Majan/ Mirjan-pa	Carpenters and masons are the same
			Mohammad Hasan S/O Qasim	-do-	
4.	Shipkun	Mason	-do-		
5.	Chempo-pa	Tailors	Raza Hussain S/O Qasim	Majan-pa	
6.	Ranthoq-pa	Millers			Self service.
7.	Thaqskan	Weavers	Jaffar	Dolthoq-pa	
			Haji Mohammad		
			Haji Mehdi	Kalbi-pa	
			Raza S/O Qasim	Majan-pa	
			Haji Ghulam Hasain	Rulba-pa	
			Ghulam	Rulba-pa	Pattoo weavers only

Looking at the above table one arrives at the following conclusions:

(a) Occupational specialisation is neither based on ethnicity nor vested with a status as a Haji may also specialise as a Lamkhan (cobbler) as in case of Haji Ibrahim and Haji Haider.

(b) One person may specialise in more than one occupation e.g., Raza S/O Qasim of Majan/Mirjan lineage is both a Champo-pa (tailor) and a Thaqskan (weaver). Sewing machines have now reduced the size of his clientels but weaving compensates for a fall in his tailor's occupation. Thus occupational diversification and mobility is rapid and frequent.

(c) Since the village Ranthoq-pa (miller) died 12 years ago, the villagers took it upon themselves to operate the village watermill. 10 to 12 families of the village assemble at the watermill, operate it and grind their foodgrains themselves.

(d) Remuneration for the services offered by the different class of artisans are paid either in cash or kind after the assigned work is completed. Hence there is no trace of the traditional Jajmani system reported elsewhere from rural India.

Social Stratification :

Social Stratification in Hardas, has no ethnic basis. Emically, there is no basis of differentiation between the various strata of the society. The only basis of hierarchy, thus, appears to be the direct descent from the Prophet Mohammad (S.A.).This is the reason why the groups with achieved status, find a place on the various wrungs of hierarchical ladder. No sooner a person of an alien faith converts to Islam, he is made and accepted as a member of the whole society. Sheikh Rahman is a case : he came to Kargil as a Buddhist orphan and was given shelter by one of the Balti families of Hardas with whom he started working as a farm hand. Subsequently, he was converted to Islam and married with his master's daughter. Though he should have found a place amongst the farmers but he was given the title of Shaikh by the villagers just as a gesture of goodwill.

The social stratification in Wakha is that of similar to Hardas as most of the villagers claimed to be Balti in origin. Since the village is divided into Buddhists and Muslims, the Mons continue to carry their old identity inspite of being converted to Islam. Wakha does not contain any Agha family but a Shaikh is there. Here the ruling family is known as Kacho.

The composite picture of social stratification that emerges from the three intensive study villages has been depicted in the following diagramme .

Ascribed		Agha or Syed — Mujtahid / Non-Muitahid	Immigrants
Zone of Group/ Occupational mobility		SHEIKH (MUJTAHID) AKHUN (NON-MUJ-TAHID PRIEST) HAJI ZAMINDAR (Rom/Raj-Shin DOM/MON (Deummers &	AUTOCTHONES OF KARGIL
Social status in Iransition		Muscians in the past; now artisans)	

It is clear from the above diagramme that achievement of higher status through Islamic learning is possible. Occupational mobility is neither decided by birth nor by tradition. A Dom has, in theory, every opportunity to become a Sheikh but since no such case was reported from Kargil, the epistemological possibility has been shown by black line and arrows. Zamindars have, in fact, become Hajis, Akhuns or Sheikhs. Hence, the direction of their group mobility between Zamindar, Haji, Akhun and Sheikh has also been shown by black arrows. The group mobility among the Muslims of Kargil is only uni-directional and upward. The reverse movement is very difficult if not possible. A Sheikh e.g., is a Zamindar also but his status as a Sheikh is primary unless he commits such offences that all his privileges as a priest get forfeited and he lives the life of a Zamindar. No such cases have been noticed anywhere in Kargil since inception of Islam though it may be true in cases of Buddhist Lamas, who, in order to avoid the rigours of monastic life and celibacy renounce the priest-hood, get married and lead a life as a member of *hinjung* (Rizvi:1987). A Muslim priest on the other hand, is very near to the life style of an ordinary man though he has to maintain a puritanic style of life. The Agha mujtahids live in a tight compartment where they have neither the freedom to go up in the hierarchy nor come down by any means. Group exogamy upward or down below also does not play any role either in enhancing or decreasing the soical status of groups ruling out further any possibility of formation of sub-groups viz., sub-castes. It is here that social stratification among the Muslims of Kargil stands in the opposite contrast to the Hindu caste model where social status of a group is fixed by virtue of an individuals' birth in a particular group. The upward group mobility is attained through hypergamy but hypogamy still remains an unthinkable proposition. The major determinants of caste system are absent from the Muslims of Kargil.

The Baltis of Hardas are divided into the following 20 lineages *(phospone)* which were endogamous in the past but now the principle of endogamy does not prevail.

Table. 11

Phosphone (lineages) among the Baltis of Hardas.

Phosphopne	Name of common ancestor	Place of origin	No. of families	Remarks
1. Rulba-pa	Rulba the weakling	?	9	Later settlers
2. Hussain Mir-pa	Hussain Mir	Sinkarmo	9	Earlier settlers
3. Majan-pa	Mohammad Jan	-do-	8 -	-do-
4. Skitali-pa	Skit Ali	-do-	7	-do-
5. Haider-pa	Haider	-do-	7	-do-
6. Ashur-pa	Ashur	Humzigund	6	-do-
7. Khache-pa	Khache- Kashmiri	Gund	6	-do-
8. Kalbi-pa	Kalbe	Sinkarmo	5	-do-
9. Ghote-pa	?	Hamzigund	3	-do-
10. Dolthoq-pa	?	-do-	3	Later settlers
11. Mala-pa	Mala	?	3	Earlier settlers
12. Syed-pa	Agha of Hardas	Kharmany	3	Later settlers
13. Arab-pa	?	?	2	-do-
14. Rehman-pa	Rehman	Skardo	2	Earlier settlers
15. Shafi-pa	Shafi	Hamzigund	2	-do-
16. Purig-pa	?	Purig	2	Late settlers
17. Darvesh-pa	Darvesh	Skardo	1	
18. Goya-pa	Goyu		1	
19. Karpo-chuli-pa	-	Hamzigund	1	Settle Hardas about yrs
20. Benmo-pa	?	?	1	Later settlers
Total			81	

It is evident from the above table that Rulbe and Hussain Mir-pa are the dominant clans of the village having nine constituent families each. Next Majan-pa are nearer to Hassain Mir and Mohammad Jan in the fifth ascending generation were collateral cousins, hence, the two lineages consisting of 17 families of the village are soically, economically, politically and emotionally are nearer to each other than the other lineages of the village. Next come Skitali -pa and Haider-pa which constitute of 7 families each. Ashur-pa and Kache'-pa have 6 families each; Kalbi-pa is constituted of 5 families; Ghote-pa, Dolthoq-pa, Mala-pa and Syeid-pa are constituted of 3 families each; Arab-pa, Rahman-pa, Shafi-pa and Purig-pa have 2 families each and the Darvesh-pa, Goya-pa, Karpo-Chuli-pa and Beumo-pa are represented in the village by one family each.

Members of a phosphone prefer to marry their children within their own phosphone in case a suitable mate is available, if not, then with the consent of phosphone's elders they seek marital unions in other phosphones. Members of phosphone act collectively on occasions like marriage, mourning and festivals. Lands in Hardas are owned by the respective phosphone who, in return, divide it amongst the constituent households according to their respective needs. The canal *(Kuhl)* water is smililarly divided by the members of respective phosphones. Each phosphone has been authorised to use the Kuhl water for an allotted period of time according to a time schedule evolved by and usually adhered to by the villagers. In event of marriage in a phosphone all its members are invited in addition to one member of the each family of the hamlet where the ceremony is performed. During festivals like Eid-e-Qurban, all members of the phosphone meet with each other, distribute the meat of the sacrificed goat or ram. The intensity of soical relations is higher in degree within a phosphone vis-a-vis other phosphones. When death occurs in a family, all members of the phosphone assemble in the deceassed's house, make arrangements for funeral, allocating the various responsibilities involved in the funerary rites: some member run to Kargil for purchase of cloth for coffin, others help to give a final bath *(ghusl-e-maiyat)* to the body whereas others dig the grave. After burial it is an obligation on the part of each member of the household of a *phosphone* to be in the company of the next of the deceased's kin. On the third day after death all member of the aggrieved phosphone take the responsibility upon themselves to offer at least a *tabaq* dish of *Khachi* and a little quantity of butter to the departed soul at the latters grave and offer *fateha.* When a body is lowered down in the grave, the elderly member of the phosphone certifies the good moral character of the deceased. This certificate *(shahadatnama)* is kept on the breast of the deceased as a witness so that he does not have to face difficulties in the other world. Thus a phosphone, members of which trace their descent with a male common ancestor, is a close-knit endogamous group characterised with the spirit of co- operation and comraderie.

Other Kin Groups:

Agnates *(phasir)* have a privileged place in the male dominated patrilineal, patrilocal and patrinymic Balti society. They are always taken into confidence on matters pertaining to negotiations, ceremonies and rituals involved in marriage, and other life cycle rituals. When a hopeless parturient mother dies after giving birth to a child, an agnates is expected to nurse the child. Usually the Fa Si comes forward as the wet-nurse of her brother's child and she virtually becomes mother of the child barring all marriage unions between her own children.

The kin related through mother (*masir*) also play significant role in the various life cycle rituals. No marriage procession in fact is completed without the presence of Momo(Mobr) and phaphi (Mobrwi/Fa Si). The kin related through wife (*skut-pa*) are treated with a measure of formality. On their arrival the traditional *cha* is replaced by the elaborate *qahwa*. The dinner in the honour of visiting *Skut-pa* is transformed into a small feast in which other close kin are also invited. A chicken dish invariably served on the *dastarkhan* (a cloth-spread on the floor on which food is served).

Family :

The nearest term defining a family is (*nang*) which is the focal point of all socio-economic activities. The *nang* is headed by father, or father's elder brother, if laterally extended or by father's father if vertically extended. All economic resources earned or acquired by the various members of the family reallocated by the family head to its various members. Before the rights and duties of the family members are described, it is apt to have a look into types of family among the Baltis of Hardas.

Table 12

Family types among the Balti of Hardas.

Sl.No.	Family type	No.	Percentage
1.	Nuclear	38	46.90
2.	Vertically extended	30	37.00
3.	Laterally extended	5	6.10
4.	Broken	8	10.00
Total		81	100.00

The above table shows the preponderane of nuclear families over compound families both vertically and laterally extended. Out of 81 families of the village 38 (46.90 per cent) were found nuclear and 35 compound. The number of vertically extended families stood 30 (37.00 per cent) and laterally extended 5 (6.10 per cent).The number of broken families was recorded 8 (10.00 per cent). The details of broken families are furnished below : 1) Mohammad's son Ali died leaving behind his widow and two minor children. The deceased wife remarried and shifted to Lota Uthalu. The children of the deceased are living with their father's father Mohammad, 2) A widow aged 60 and her daughter aged 19, 3) Ghulam Mehdi living with his two minor sons, 4) Rajab living with his minor son, 5) Amina living with her minor son, 6) Syed Haider living with two of his students, 7) Hadi living with his father and four daughters whose ages ranged between 8 to 16 years.

Father is the sole authority in the family even in the families of three generations depth. Haji Ghulam (65 years) is the father of Sheikh Hasan, the *mujtahid* priest. In all matters of religious significance Sheikh Hasan had a last say but in secular spheres of day to day family affairs the voice of Haji Ghulam was considered final. Haji Ghulam himself served as Army Numberdar for considerable period of time. He was a proud father of an accomplished priest that remains a dream of every Shia Muslim of Kargil who resorts to hard labour in or outside Kargil in places like Simla, Dehra Dun, Mussoorie, Chakaata, Ambala, Saharanpur and even Chandigarh (Rizvi: 1977) just in order to earn enough to send at least one of their male children to Karbula-e-Maulla, Najaf Asharaf or Qum to become an accomplished priest and when he returns to his respective village it is great moment of rejoicing for the father. The Islamic system of values lays a great stress on familial relationships. Each category of relationship has been elaborately defined. Since the Muslims of Kargil have a greater degree of conformity to the Islamic tenets, they follow the Islamic code of conduct in its true spirit and content. This statement should not be considered as a subjective but this observation is largely based on strong empirical realities as prevailed in Kargil. Women too do not lag behind in performance of their family obligations. Their main responsibility is not only to procreate and raise the children but to keep the house and hearth warm when the temperature touches down an arctic-25^{0} celsius. Their summers are spent either in the field or on the desolate heights of mountains in gleaning animals dropping and juniper bushes. The elderly ladies take charge of looking after the young. Winter is a real test for their fortitude when the able bodied male members of the family remain away in unknown lands for about 5 to 6 months in a stretch. Then comes 21st March, the day that heralds the new year, Navroz, an occasion of great festivities for the Shia Muslims of Kargil. Navroz not only announces the beginning of a new year ahead but also of the responsibilities that lay ahead in the coming year, when fields still remain snow-locked and snow storms lash the redoubtable peaks and the sun is yet to release its warmth from its womb, the women come out from the warm cosiness of their homes to fight a grim battle with the elements of nature for their survival. Equipped with a conical wicker basket and a spade they manure their snow-locked fields allowing the snow to melt prematurely by the heat accumulated by the dust particles from the feeble March sun rays.

The fission of a joint family was found to be more a result of the developmental cycle of a domestic group rather than a result of modernization or industrialization harbouring individualistic out look leading to conflict and confrontation leading to the fission of familial unit.

The Balti Kinship Terms :

The Balti kinship terminology has a Buddhist infusion of terms. There is only a negligible difference in the respective kinship terminologies of Hardas and Wakha, Hence the kinship terminologies of the two villages would be dealt together, however, differences, if any, would be brought to relief.

The Denotative Terms :

The terms of reference to wife are 'bustring' and 'Zangse' whereas she is addressed by a term 'le'. The term of reference for husband on the other hand, is *'ashepa'* or *'daq-pa'* and the term of address is the same 'le'. In Wakha the term of address is 'me'. Mother's brother is referred to and addressed as 'Momo'; Mo Br Wi is 'ane'. In Hardas the term of reference for father is 'ata' and term of address is 'aba'. The term of reference for mother is 'amo' and term of address 'ama'. The term of address for Da Hu is 'asho' and term of reference 'makpa'. 'Ache' is the elder sister and 'Nono' is the younger. Mother and mother's sister are called by the same term 'amo'. Zho is the term for Mo Br So, Da So, So So, Br So and Zhomo for mother's brothers daughter, sister (younger), daughter's daughter, son's daughter and brother's daughter. Here one may note that the criterian of generation has been ignored as all younger boys have been brought together under the 'Zho' and younger girls are zhomo or chomo. 'Ata' is father, father's brother and father's sister's husband. Male members of the second descending generation like son, sister's son, brother's son etc. are referred to as and addressed as 'bu'. The criterian of affinity is also ignored as father's father and mother's father are referred to by the same term 'apa' and father's mother and mother's mother are referred to by the same term 'api'. 'Mene' is the term for wife's sister, father's sister, wife's brother's wife, father's brother's wife and wife's younger sister.

The spouses use the same kinship terms for each other's kin as they use for their own kin. 'Apang' is the term for sister's husband and father's sister's husband. One may notice that the criterian of generation is ignored in this case. Father's father's father is 'apo' ameshpo' and father's father's mother is 'api' 'mashpo'.

The criterion of relative age is maintained by suffixing 'chogho' (elder) and 'chunse' (younger): father's elder brother is 'apa chogho' and father's younger brother 'apa'chunse'.The nature of interpersonal relationships have already been described at various places in this report and still there is a scope to describe them at various stages of the life cycle, hence they do not warrant an exclusive description here. There is nothing particular or peculiar in way of kinship usages as none of them is really in vogue either in the case of the Baltis of Hardas or of Wakha.

Birth of a child is an occasion of happiness with a subdued sense of joy in case of daughters. A male child makes the parents proud. A room in the house is given to the parturient mother on the onset of throes. A comfortable hay-bed covered with *chari* bedstead is made in a corner of the room. An elderly lady of the house assisted by other experienced ladies of the village help the partuient mother in delivery. The umblical cord is cut by a sharp-edged knife by the ladies attending the mother. The placenta and after birth is buried in a corner of the house. The parturient mother is served with sweetened tea (*lipton-cha*) before the delivery. After birth she is immediately given brackish tea seasoned with butter. This child is given first bath in lukewarm water immediately after birth. The Sheikh of Akhun recites 'aza:n' in both the ears of the new-born.

Nosh-yoni :

The mother takes bath after seven days. A feast is given by the father of the new-born in which all members of the blessed couple's linage participate offering them seven baked breads. The offering of the baked breads which is considered as the sign of fertility in the Bonist tenets but survived in the Balti custom even after their conversion to Islam. The pre-Buddhist Bon deity Keisar and Brugma were implored for granting children by offering seven images of ibex made of wheat flour. This practice continued even in Buddhist era. After the advent of Islam, which strictly prohibited all forms of idolatory, the seven flour ibex images were transformed into seven leavened breads. The occasion coincides with *aqeeqa* i.e. the obligatory shaving of the child's hair and sacrifice of a goat or ram. The consanguinal kin of the child do not eat the meat of the sacrificed animal, but the same is distributed among the needy and deserving non-kin of the neonats or else is sent to an orphanage.

Name Giving :

The process of giving a name to the newly born is as follows: The Sheikh or Akhun opens a page of Holy Quran amidst incantation of prayers. The first alphabet starting the first word on the left page is thus picked up for the name to be given to the new born child. The names are after the names of the Prophets, and the member's of his household (*ahle bait*) and close companions (*ansaar*). Similarly girls are given names based on the name of mother and wives of various Prophets and their close kin. Some of the names especially in case of girls have been abbreviated prochialised viz., Khati, from Khadija (.S.A.)- Prophet Mohammad's wife : Phati, from Fatima (S.A.)- Prophet Mohammad's daughter and Saki from Sakina (S.A.) Imam Hussain's daughter. Similarly in case of men Male stands for Mohammad Ali; Majan for Mohammad Jan.

On the 40th day after birth the mother is given another bath (*ghusl-e-nifaas*) that removes all pollutants from her body. After this bath she resumes her normal demostic duties. On an auspicious day the new born child is taken to the roof-top with two plates of cooked food. Members of father's *phosphon* invite the blessed couple and give feasts in their honour celebrating the arrival of a new member in the lineage.

Age at Marriage :

The average age at marriage is 20 years for boys and for a girl 17 or 18 years. Early marriages are unknown. The boys and girls have no freedom to choose a life partner according to their sweet will. The amount of *mehr*, the guarantee money paid by the groom's side to the bride, is relatively very high, almost the highest in the area, which ranges between Rs. 5000/- to Rs. 10,000/-. The mutually agreed upon amount of *mehr* is payable in cash.

Rules of Marriage :

Marriage within a *phosphon* is allowed between father's brother's sister and father's brother's son. Cross cousin marriages are generally allowed but marriage alliances between the maternal parallel cousins are not allowed. The prohibited categories of marriage are as follows :

(a) between siblings from the common parents,

(b) between children of a mother who has acted as a wet nurse for a child other than her own,

(c) marriage with a non-Muslim excepting Christians and Jews in principle but no such cases were recorded from Kargil.

Buddhists, though non-Muslims, may be considered for marriage alliances only after conversion to Islam. In some cases it has been observed that the two spouses have retained their original faiths even after conversion. Such cases occur in those areas where numerically weaker Muslim population merges with the majority Buddhist population. The religious affiliations of the off-spring is decided by a compromise which envisages the male offsprings to follow their father's religion and the female their mother's.

Types of Marriage :

Islam prohibits polyandry as a sinful practice. The change over from one system of marriage that entailed polyandry to the Islamic system with polygynous overtones, put conjungal ties under tremendous strains as the pre-Islamic or Buddhist type of polyandrous marriages was well suited to the ecological situation prevailing in Kargil. Consequently, the Muslims of Kargil adopted a system of marriage which was much more convenient to them because of its greater flexibility. This new system early evolved in Arabia was handed down to the people of Kargil by their Arabian predecessors.

Marriage is treated as a social contract in the Muslim law. Sexual relation between the members of the opposite sex are limited within its confines. The core of marriage rituals is ***nikah*** which consists of incantation of holy verses *(segha)* and obtaining the consent of the two prospective spouses in the presene of two witnesses (***Wakil***) on a pre-determined amount of guarantee money (***mehr***) payable to the bride by the bride groom on demand. Termination of ***nikah*** union is possible when the conjugal relations between the two spouses get ruptured beyond repairs. This type of marriage may be termed as ***bakhstan*** (negotiated marriage) with permanent marriage contract (***nikah-e-daimi***).

The other type of marriage, known as ***mutah*** or ***nikah-e- inqatai*** is a temporary marriage contract. It may be settled by negotiation (***bakhstan***) or may be performed secretly (***khuftan***). The marriage alliance in case of ***mutah*** is terminable at will of the male spouse. ***Mutah*** qualifies a man to marry with a lady of his choice for a stipulated period of time which varies between few hours to 100 years. Succession of property is the only factor that differentiates the two systems. In case of ***nikah-e-daimi*** a husband has a claim on the property of his wife at the rate of 50.00 per cent if he is issueless or 25.00 per if he has issues. Correspondingly a female spouse has also a right on her husband's 1/4th of portion of property if she is issueless and 1/8th portion if she is with issues. A widow, however, has no right on her deceased husband's property unless otherwise willed by the latter in favour of the former but in case of ***nikah-e-inqatai*** or ***mutah*** neither of the two have a right on each other's property. The husband, however, is fully responsible for the maintenance of his wife and children, if any, for the entire period of the contractual marriages obligation. In the event of termination of *mutah* he is responsible for maintenance and upbringing of children till the time they become self-supporting.

Ahluwalia (1980 :126) also refers to temporary or short contract marriages as *mutah* which he found prevalent in Kashgar where, the duration of such unions, according to him, was minutes or hours. The present study showed the frequency of *mutah* marriages as 98.83 per cent and the stipulated duration of *mutah* unions were found varying between 20 years to 100 years with the price of *mehr* ranging between Rs. 28/- to Rs. 100.00.

The factors responsible for the high frequency of *mutah* in Kargil may be enumerated as below :

(a) Ecological Factors :

There is a strong evidence to suggest that *mutah* was prevalent in Islamic Arabia. Zaidi (1965) is of the view that "*mutah* has saved thousands from adultery, a sinful practice that invites punishment : a male offender gets 100 lashes and a female is liable to be stoned to death. Alltama Zamakhshari, Qazi Baizavi and Fakhruddin Raazi have quoted verses from Quran in support of *mutah* as a legal form of marriage. There are innumerable traditions (*ahadis*) which prohibit *mutah* with a lady of doubtful character. Imam jafar-e-Sadiq (A.S.) is being quoted to have said that the *mutah* is illegal with a debauch woman".

The system of *mutah* came to stay in Arabia as a process of ecological adaptation. The arid or semi-arid situation that existed in Arabia also existed in Kargil. The social structure of pre-Islamic Arabia was largely composed of several tribal groups sharing a common ecological niche and always at war with each other in order to gain a politico-economic dominance over the scarce resources existing in the arid deserts. Harsh climate and scarce means of livlihood forced the Arabian nomads to keep the size of their bands to a bare minimum level necessitating frequent female infanticide. Anotherreasons behind this practice was the low status of women in a predominantly patriarchal society in which they were considered as unwanted. The practice of female infanticide resulted into scarcity of female population. This led to forceful induction of female members in a tribe from other tribal groups. Thus the tribal settlements would be raided and women would be taken away as the priced booty. Men, on the other side, were required to fight and defend their bands whereas women were considered as 'deficient in wisdom' *(naqis-ul-aql)*, and a virtual burden on the groups to whom they belonged.

After the advent of Islam the lot of women was considerably improved; female infanticide was prohibited and the women were given the right to own property. Wars, however, still continued for expanding the new faith. Since agriculture was an unthinkable proposition amidst arid deserts, trade continued to be the main source of livelihood in the post-Islamic Arabia necessitating men to stay away from their homes for longer periods of time and thus the idea of short term contract marriages (*mutah*) was evolved at that stage.

In Kargil, the pressure on land is tremendous and agriculture had never been a viable source of livelihood. Surrounded by lofty Himalayan peaks, Kargil receives scant rainfall. Polyandry, thus, emerged as a well suited type of marriage in the harsh climate of Laddakh. It provided not only extra hands to work but also saved limited size of landholding from futher uneconomic fragmentation. Besides polyandry, the lamaist system, with a strong emphasis on primogeniture, was also evolved to keep the economy in a good shape; inbreeding among the Buddhist population helped to keep the population at a lower level. After Kargil became Muslim, it had to cope up with the problem of increasing population and decreasing size of landholdings. Thus, trade emerged as a viable alternative. After stoppage of trade activities due to emergence of a new alien rulers across the border the need to defend the national borders became imperative and thus the local people were compensated the deficient agriculture with wage labour. This also necessitated men to remain out of their homes for long periods. Lest they fall pray to adultery, *mutah* appeared as a convenient tool for satisfaction of their sexual urges while remaining away from home.

(b) Fundamental Flexibility :

Permanent marriage contract (*nikah-e- daimi*) is more rigid in comparision to temporary marriage contract (*mutah*)as the former bestows the right of ownership of property to the spouse and divorce is difficult to obtain. In event of divorce, the guarantee money is to be paid in full by the divorcing husband to his wife. If the lattter wishes to seek divorce, she will have to exempt her maintenance. Consent of both the spouses is essential in case of divorce which is finally given effect by a priest in the presence of the respective representatives of the two spouses. Remarriage of the two divorcing spouses is not allowed until the divorced wife performs *hajala* which necessitates her to remarry with another man and seek a decree of divorce enabling her to remarry with her first husband.

Mutah on the other hand, is more flexible in practice and approach. The amount of *mahr* remains low though the duration of *mutah* may be as long as 100 years but the husband has the right to terminate the contract earlier also if he wishes to do so after the payment of *mahr* and accepting the responsibility of the maintenance of children.

Secret *mutah* unions (*Khuftan*) without prior public approval are frowned and looked down upon. A priest of Wakha had a widowed cousin living with him. She was found pregnant after living sometimes in the house of the said priest. This episode attracted the attention of the villagers and the matter was brought before the Goba, the traditional village council. The guilty woman was called before the Goba where she openly confessed to carry the said priest's child. The priest in his statement said that he had taken the lady to wedlock after peforming *mutah* secretly. Further, he took upon himself the responsibility for the maintenance of his wife and the child yet to be born. The said priest was physically handicapped. He therefore, did not like to take the villagers into confidence lest he become a laughing stock but in the process he eventually invited the attention of the Goba and earned a public ridicule.

Changing System of Marriage:

After independence from the Shakhsi hukoomat of the Dogara rulers the economy of the people got a considerable boost owing to the land reforms and expansion of communication and defence network. The newly earned wealth was mainly invested in bringing about a socio-religious reform in Kargil. Villagers despatched their children abroad at an early age of 12 to 13 years to the Islamic *madarasas* for advanced training in Shiite theology. The earliest badge of thus fully accomplished priests returned to Kargil in early sixties. This new generation of priests were of the view that though *mutah* is a vaild type of marrriage but it should be avoided and emphasis should be laid increasingly on permanent marriage contract (*nikah-e-daimi*). An enlightened priest of Hardas returned form Iraq to his village as a bachelor. He opted for *nikah-a-daimi* not only for himself but for his younger siblings too. Thus the religious elite are now putting a greater emphasis on *nikah-e-daimi*.

Among the Shias of other parts of India, the *mutah* system has become a vestige of the feudal past. Even in the Kashmir valley the Shias have no fascination for *mutah*. With the increasing spread of education and job opportunities it is hoped that *mutah* marriages will gradually decrease if not completely given up.

Cousin Marriages:

There is neither any prescription nor any restriction on parallel or cross-cousin marriages. The following genealogical diagramme of Haji Ghulam Hussian of Hardas makes it amply clear.

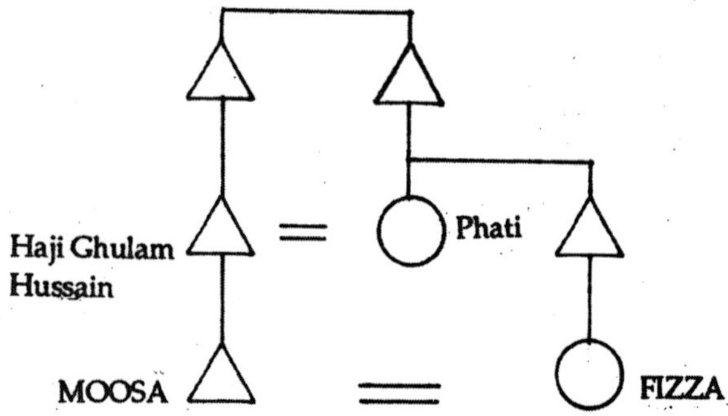

In the above diagramme, Ego Haji Ghulam Hussain is married to Phati, his father's brothers daughter whereas their son Moosa married with Fizza who is Phati's decased brother's daughter.

(C) Haji Haider's son Ali of Majdaz is married with Khati, his father's sister's daughter. This may be diagrammitically represented as under:

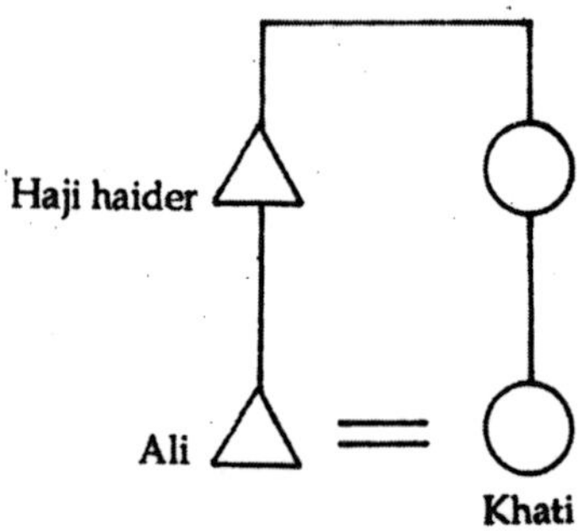

Out of the 9 cases of cousin marriages, in 4 cases Ego married to father's sister's daughter and in the remaining two cases the ego married with mother's brother's daughter. Hence it appears that the Baltis of Hardas put more emphasis on marrying with father's brother's and sister's daughters in comparison to mother's brother's daughters which is per in accordance with a strong patrilineal bias of the Balti society.

Levirate:

Levirate, both senior as well as junior is allowed in order to meet family obligations. Let us have a look at the following diagramme :

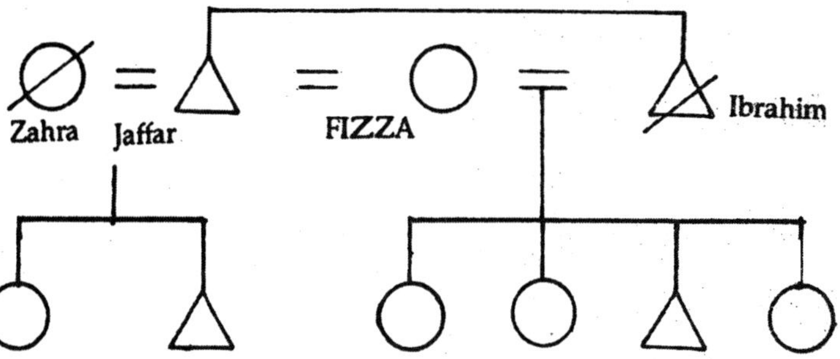

Ego Jaffar had a brother Ibrahim who was younger to him Jaffar was married to Zahra and bore two children. Jaffar divorced his wife who left children behind and married elsewhere. Jaffar was leading a widower's life. His younger brother Ibrahim, who was a labourer, got killed accidentally. He left his widow Kulsum and four children. Jaffar subsequently married with Kulsum.

Similarly a case of senior levirate was also recorded from Hardas. It may be presented as below:

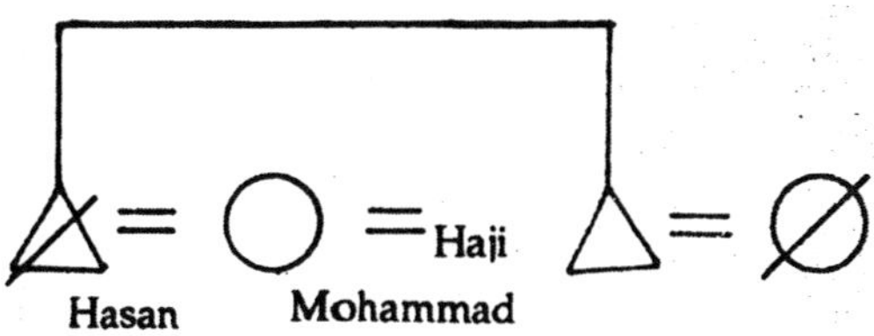

Ego Haji Md. after his wife's death married with the widow of his decsased brother Hasan. No cases of sororate came to the notice of this author in the study villages.

Methods of Acquiring Mates :

There are basically three methods of acquiring mates in Kargil which are as under :

(a) Marriage by negotaition *(Bakhstan)*

(b) Marriage by service (*Shiendepf*) or Makpa

(c) Marriage by exchange *(Parboti)*

Marriage by negotiation:

Marriage by negotiation is largely an accepted method of marriage for which the Balti have a term *bakhstan.* The various stages and rituals involved in *bakhstan* are described below:

The qualification of the prospective grooms are as follows : he should own some landed property, should be of high morality and conviction (*iman*) and should also be free from bodily defects and deformities. For girls: higher degree of morality and conviction (*iman*) less demanding, gentle and full of humility: personal merits of a girl are considerd more improtant than the property she owns.

The negotiation for marriage are invariably started by a mediator (*halpa*) who should be cleaver, pursuasive and secretive. Haji Ali and Hussain of Hardas play this role in the village. Husain had successfully arranged three marriages in the village. Arranging marriages is an act that accrues merit (*sawab*). Hence a *halpa* neither demands nor is paid any remuneration for his services. He also does not undertake any guarantee for success of a marriage alliance.

The parents of the prospective groom send the *halpa* to prospective bride's family with cash money ranging between Rs. 1/-toRs 10/- for the groom's parents with a request to fix up a date for marriage. The bride's father gives a date for his daughter's marriage as per his covenience after consulting the Sheikh. In case there is a fear that the father of the bride is in a hurry for his daughter's marriage, all customary marriage rituals, are deferred and only *nikah* (segha) is solemnised. The girl continues to stay with her parents until the completion of customary marriage rituals. In such an eventuality after *nikah* ceremony the grooms side offers sweets to Imams (*nazar*) and distribute them among the various members of the grooms lineage. Dry apricots are also distributed on this occasion in the bride's family. Tea is served to the members of the lineage. The bride-groom and the bride are not perimitted to meet with one another unless all formalities of marriage are completed.

Halpa also negotiates the amount of guarantee money (*mahr*) on behalf of the father of the bride-groom about which a fromal consent is taken from the bride-groom at the time of Nikah.

Nikah :

Nikah is solemnised by the Sheikh, who goes first to the girl's house, and asks the bride, "Are you, the daughter of so and so, ready to marry with (name of the bridegroom) son of so and so on a predetermined and known *mahr* of rupees (the amount fixed earlier)?" The bride should say' yes'. The same words are repeated three times and the bride gives her consent each time. After seeking the consent from the bride the Shekih goes to the house of the bridegroom and extracts thrice a similar consent from him. Thereafter, he incants the prascribed *segha* verses in the presence of *halpa* and other kin of the bride and the bridegroom. The guests and relatives of the two sides are entertained by the respective sides. Soon after *nikah* a date is fixed for *bakhstan* by the Sheikh on the request of the groom's father. The bride's father is also consulted about fixation of date through the *halpa.* One day before marriage the bridegroom's father sends the following articles to the bride: butter - 1 kg., *pattoo* cloth (as per demand of the bride's father) and one or two pairs of clothes and foot-wears for the bride. The *halpa* sends 30 piece of leavened breads as his contribution, which, are distributed among the near kin of the bride. Halpa returns with some cash (ranging beweeen Rs. 1/- to Rs 30/-) in the same container in which he has sent the breads earlier.

Thazan :

In the evening, all members of the bridegroom's *phosphon* (lineage) and other near relatives are entertained with a feast in which flour of parched barley *(khachi)*,butter,rice, vegatable, mutton, breads, boiled or dry apricots and sweetened *(lipton-cha)* or salted tea *(cha)* are served to the guests.

The guests consist of all members of the hamlet in which a marriage is performed and the head of family or his representative in addition to all cognates from other hamlets. If one can afford one can invite the entire population of the village. After *thazan,* all excepting cognates, disperse. The congates are served with a meal thereafter.

The bridegroom *(baq-pa)* is given a bath by *chasis pa* (the close associates and friends of the groom) who take the responsibility of the looking after the needs of the bridegroom during the marriage in the afternoon. In return the *chasis pa* receive clothes of the *baq-pa* as the latter puts on new clothes after taking the ceremonial bath. Done in his finery the *baq-pa* enters the sitting room where Agha, the Shekikh, the Akhun and all other guests assemble, The Agha or Sheikh recites holy prayers over a cup of water which is sprinkled on the clothes of the bridegroom. Sweet is distributed among the guests. Thereafter, poems in praise of *Chaharde Masoomin* (The Fourteen Innocents) are recited. The bridegroom, then, is taken in a procession consisting of halpa, *chasis-pa* and 3 or 4 agnates, to the brides house. In the past the Doms used to play music in the front of the marriage procession but now the Agha and Sheikh *mujtahids* have banned the practice of playing music as an un-Islamic practice. Bridegroom's parents abstain from prticipating in the marriage procession.

After the procession reaches near the bride's house, the members of the procession seek the permission of the village elders to enter into the bride's house and fetch the bride. The procession is received by the bride's near kin and the bride is brought from inside the house with her companions (*mome*) and the nikah ceremony is performed in the night at the bridegroom's place. The *segha* is read by a *mujtahid* priest or his chosen representative in the presence of two *wakils* each representing the bride's and the bridegroom's side. Thereafter, the bridegroom and his parents go to the brides villages to bring her back to her husband's village. Then she is taken to the groom's house where she is received by the latter's kin. The guests are served with sweet tea and a feast is given in the night *(ishanamizaan)* in the honour of the bride's relatives. Boiled rice steamed flour of parched barley (*khachi*), butter, mutton, vegetables, pudding and sweet tea and tobacco etc. are served in the feast. The bride's people except the *momo*, return to their village on the next day. Two days after the groom (*baq-pa*), the bride (*baq-mo*) and *momo* and the parents of the bridegroom go to the bride's house where a ceremonial feast (*slum*) in given to them.

The bride brings with her a set of bedding consisting of a carpet (*dari*), a mattresss, a quilt and a bed sheet ; patto, 1 to 3 pairs of clothes, foot-wear, utensils, crockery, bronze or copper tumblers and a *lota* vessel.

The bride's parents give a feast (*khansgo*) to the bridegroom and his parents. The bride's kin make gift of clothes, sheep and goats to the couple. The groom and his parents return to their village leaving behind the bride who continues to stay for another month with her parents. Thereafter, she returns to her husband and stays there permanently in the village (shoure).

Marriage by Service :

Marriage by servivce or *makpa* is another prevalent type of marriage in Kargil. The term *makpa* means daughter's husband in Bodhi hence the same term is used in Hardas and Wakha for such marriages. Men also stay in the house of their respective wives or in their wife's father's house having an uxhorilocal mode of residence.

Absence of a male issue is the prime motive behind a *makpa* marriage which entitles a female issue to own and inherit the family property. Thus, a father partly due to his affection for his only daughter does not want to part her company after her marriage and since she is the potential heir of the property her chance of getting a *makpa* becomes brighter.

Widows or divorcee owning land may also take resort to *makpa* marrriage. In some cases the age difference between the wife and husband was found to be 10 to 12 years otherwise the normative pattern is that wife should be younger in age than her husband. Asked as to why the age disparity is allowed in case of *makapa* marriage, the explanation given was that there are better chances of having less number of children if the wife is senior in age than her husband. *Moraso*, a *makpa* is invariably a landless person without any proper means of livlihood. Hence he has very limited options of his own.

The right of property in case of *makpa* vests with the wife and after her death to her children. The husband is entitled only for a specified portion of his wife's property after death. Thus the status of a *makpa* is neither at par with the *bakhstan nor with kash*, in the latter the husband being the virtual master of his household by virtue of the ownership of immovable family property. Socially, also *makpa* marriages are performed more as a compulsion rather by one's own willingness. This attitude is responsible for a lower frequency of *makpa* unions. The frequency of makpa marriages was found 5.87 per cent.

The following case study stated below make the motives behind *makpa* marriages still clearer :

> Badruddin came to Hardas from Iraq. During his stay in the village he performed *mutah* with a Balti woman and returned to Iraq leaving behind his daughter Nargis whose mother also died when she was 12 years old. Nargis having lost both parents now was being looked after by her remote kin. When she attained marriageable age the villagers looked around for a suitable match for her. Incidentally a Buddhist boy came from Pheyong and settled down in Wakha. The villagers converted him to Islam and named him as Sheikh Salman. The title of Sheikh was given to him as a special gesture lest he feels uneasy in the village as an outside stranger. Subcequently he was married with Nargis and since then lived in the village happily with his wife and three children.

Marriage by Exhange : (Schendepff/Perboti)

Conservation of land again is the main motive behind marriage by exchange for which the Balti speaking Muslims have a term *schendepf* the *Brok-pa-parboti.* Two cases of *schendepf* were recorded at Hardas, which are described below:

Case No. 1: This case relates to *schendepf* between the two lineage Majanpa and Kalbipa as portrayed in the following diagramme :

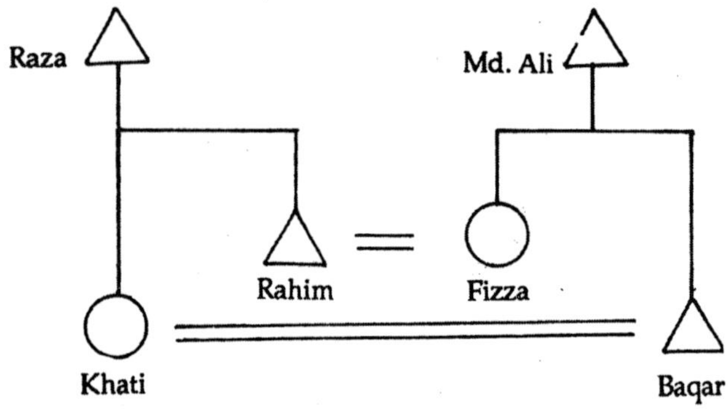

In the above diagramme Raza of Majanpa lineage has a son Rahim and a daughter Khati(Khatija). On the other hand, Mohammad Ali of Kalbi-pa lineage too has a son Baqar and a daughter Fizza. Baqar married with Khati and Fizza married with Rahim.

Case No. 2 : In this case the exchange of brides occurs in the same lineage between the children of three brothers.

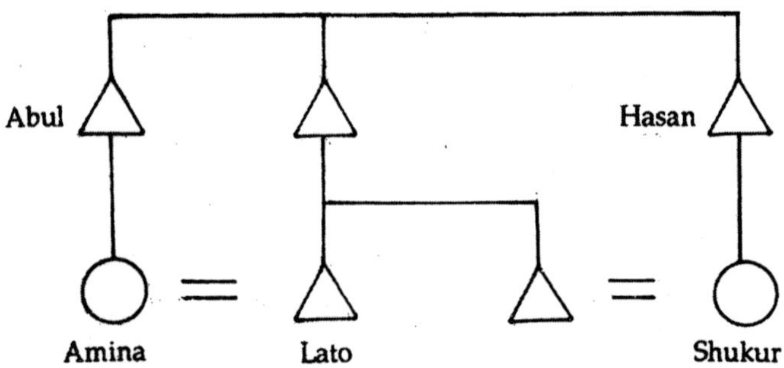

The three brothers as shown in the above diagramme lives in Dopithang, an outlying hamlet of the village. Abul married his daughter Amina with Lato, the son of his younger brother whereas his younger brother marries his younger brother Hussain. The youngest brother Hassan married his daughter Shukur Bi with son of his elder brother.

The above case falls only marginally as the case of marriage by exchange as the sibling from the parents have not exchanged but a pool of parallel cousin have been exchanged in the three marriage alliances. Hence this case may be referred to as the marriage by a pool exchange.

Levirate :

Levirate is permissible but it is practised only in order to meet certain family obligation and rehabilitation of the brother's widow and her children.

A case of junior levirate from Hardas was noticed under abnormal and tragic circumstance. A person was found murdered on the roadside. The deceased left behind his wife and two young children. The deceased's younger brother who was still a bachelor married with the widow of his deceased elder brother.

Haya Bi of Wakha is 12 years senior to her husband. The intention of having less number of children in order to check the fragmentation of land is supposed to be the cause in age disparity between the two spouses.

Sororate :

No cases of sororate were repoted as the motive behind sororate is to make good the loss of the bride price. In the event of the death of a married woman, her younger sister is offered to the agggrieved husband. Since there is no custom of paying bride price among the Muslims of Kargil the prevalence of sororate may be easily ruled out.

Remarriage :

Remarriage is possible under the following conditions in event of the death or divorce from the husband.

1. If the husband dies without his wife having conceived, the latter can remarry four months and ten days after the death of her first husband. Such a period of abstinance from marriage is known as *idda.*

2. If the husband dies leaving behind his wife pregnant, the period of *idda* will be observed untill the delivery of the said child.

3. In the event of divorce the remarriage may take place after two consecutive periods of mensruation. Such a woman can remarry after the onset of the third consecutive mensruation.

4.

If a girl is married but has not undergone the wedlock, she need not observe *idda*.

5. In event of cessession of menstruation before menopause if a woman has cohabited with her husband then she has to observe three lunar months as the period of *idda*.

6. If a husband has freed his wife before the stipulated time of *mutah*, such woman can remarry after two consecutive pariod of mensuration.

Since marriage is considered as a social contract in Islam the divorce is permissible especially in view of the Shia Muslims conformity to *mutah* system of marriage but divorce is not possible among the Muslims of Kargil by verbal pronouncement of "talaq" thrice.

Divorce :

When the conjugal ties get ruptured beyond repairs a decree of divorce is granted by the religious clergy only by obtainng the consent of the two partners and then issues his verdict for divorce. Divorce is however considered illegal during mensuration. Only men have the right to divorce but women can seek separation on specific ground.

Irreqular Marriage Alliances :

Extra-marital relations are considered as sinful. Adultery is punishable offence in the Islamic laws. Hence no cases of extra-marital sexual relations were reported from Kargil. The peopel's high degree of conformity to Islamic laws precludes the chances fo extra-marital relations.

The Last Journey :

Death is considered as a natural phenomenon. When a person dies the mourners receite a verse from the Holy Quran : Inna Iillah - e- wainna alaih-e-rajoon' meaing "one coming from Allah will return to Him" When someone dies the villagers organise themselves into two groups : one of them starts digging a grave and the other group takes upon itself the task of giving a bath to the dead body (*ghusl-a-maiyat*).

When a man dies his body is put on a wooden plank which is kept over the running *Kuhl* water. A canopy is erected over the body so that women and children do not see the dead body while it is being undressed. In fact, all the inquisitive children are driven away from the scene. Women also are not to be seen around.

It takes about half an hour to give the bath to the body strictly in accordance with *shara*. The Sheikh presides over this ritual. Holding a book in his hand he reads out passage containing necessary instructions how the bath should be given. After giving bath, the body is covered with a black cotton sheet and brought inside the *matamsara*. The Akhun prepares the shroud that consists of *Kurtani*-a shirt (unsewed) covering the body form waist to knee, *sando*-a lion cloth covering the body from abdomen to feet, *that* - a scarf covering the head and finally a white piece of cloth fully covering the body. Thereafter, the body is brought near the grave and prayer for the dead (*namaz-e-janaza*) is held.

All the above mentioned rituals are performed in a hushed silence, the villagers look at each other with cacant and sad eyes. People talk to one another only through gestures and whispers. Women too, in a corner of *matamsara* sit silently and shocked. The pent up emotions get unleashed when a villager starts reciting a dirge (*marsia*) in Balti language highlighting the martyrdom of Hazrat Ali Akbar, the eighteen year old son of Hazrat Imam Hussian in the battle of Karbala, in event of deceased's being a youth or narrating the suffering of Iman Hussian. Hearing the dirge, a hoarse chorus of human voices rents the air for a couple of minutes then it ebbs down slowly. Women beat their faces and breasts with both hands. Every one present in the crowd irrespective of age and sex weep bitterly and loudly. After recitation of *marsia* is over, the face of body is opened for the last homage. First of all the father of deceased, if alive, is brought near the body and is quickly withdrawn from the scene,then comes the brother and sisters of the deceased to see the face of their departed brother for the last time. They too are quickly withdrawn and then other villagers come one by one and return after seeing the face of the deceased. The pit dug for grave is 7 feet long, 4 1/2 ft. wide and 5 ft. deep. The inner chamber is 6 into 4 and nearly 3 feet deep. Before the body is lowered down, four people jump into the inner pit in order to give support to the body. Similarly, four persons stand in the middle chamber. After the body is laid to rest all those who entered inside the grave come out of the pit. Two green twigs are put on the right and the left side of the body. A *shahadatnama*, testifying the good conduct of the deceased is placed on the breast of the decased. Names of the heads of family of the villege are written on *shahadatnama* as witnesses to the good moral character of the deceased. The body is laid straight on the back facing west. Three stone slabs put horizontally seal the inner chamber of the grave. The crevices on the roof of the inner chamber of the grave are carefully sealed by inserting small stones here and there and the roof is plastered with mud. After sealing the inner chamber, the men come out. All those present in the crowd throw a handful of stone pebbles and dust filling the exterior chamber of the grave each time reciting 'inna lillah-e-wainna alaih-e-rajaoon!. When the pit is filled up the stone are set in order to give a shape to the grave. The crowd of mourners then slowly gets dispersed. The hearth of a home where the death has occured remains silent on the day. Hence, the members of the lineage cook food and send to the house where the tragedy has occured.

In the evening *namaz* prayers are held again in the honour of the departed soul and the deceased's father sacrifices a goat, the mutton is distributed among the villagers.

If a woman dies, all funerary rituals are performed by the elderly ladies of the *phosphon* concerned.

On the third day of the death an assembly is held in the house of the deceased. Each participant recites at least one *surah* from the Holy Quran in the honour of the departed soul. All members of the deceased's lineage send one kilogram of flour of parched barley and 250 gms. butter. Other families in the village also contribute 1.5 kgs. of the flour of the parched barley and a little amount of butter each on the grave of the deceased as an offering. The pooled itmes are in return, distributed by the deceased's father among the needy and deserving widows, orphans and invalids of the village having no source of livelihood. In the evening the priests and elders of the village assemble in the house of the deceased and are offered meals.

On the fortieth day after death a larger feast is arranged in which one family member from the each household of the father's and mother's lineage is invited. After recitation of the Holy Quran (*Quran Khani*), a *majlis* is held and meal is served to the mourners. In the evening the near kin of the deceased visit the grave, light candles and incense and offer *fatiha.* Alms are destributed among the needy and deserving persons of the villages.

Restrictions and Taboos :

For one year marriage will not be performed in a house where the death has occured. Festivals like Id-ul-Fitra and Navroz etc. will be observed with due solemnity sans festivities and rejoicings.

Religion and the Life Cycle:

It has been said earlier that religion is more a way of life for the Balti than merely a cannon of faith. The lives of the Prophets and his immediate kin are the main source of solace for the mourners. In the event of death, tragedy of Karbala overshadows all personal tragedies. People cry silently or remain silent when a person dies but they give a full vent to their pent up emotions only when a *marsia* highlighting the sufferings of the Karabala martyres, is recited. The overt expression of grief; beating of head and breast, scratching of hair etc. is less directly the outcome of the personal tragedy of death of a single individual than the group martyredom of Karbala which, naturally evokes much more sympathy and an intense emotional expression of grief amidst the mourners. Hence no tragedy is worst than the tragedy of Karbala. This is how the Balti mourn the death of one of their near and dear ones. Thus the basis of collective solidarity of the Shia Muslims of Kargil in the cycle of their lives is centred around the life, acts sayings and sufferings of the fourteen innocents.

Socio-Cultural Links Across the Border :

The Balti are divided between the two nations. They are very few in the Indian side of the line of actual control as their major concentration remains acrosss the border in Skardo, a sub- division of the erstwhile Laddakh district, which now remains under the illegal occupation of Pakistan. Many a Balti families living in Hardas are thus divided between the two countries. The interaction of the people of Hardas acrosss the border does not really exist as the people are unable to cross the border and meet with each other. Linguistic ties however, run across the border. Balti is the linguafranca of Baltistan. The Broq-pa, though have their own Shino dialect but have no script of their own hence they depend on Balti script which is Persian in character. The Muslims of Kargil have not adopted the Bodhi script which is Prakritic in character. Thus Balti serves as the main language of the Muslims of Kargil.

The people of Hardas as well as Karkit were seen thronging around the radio sets when a broadcast in Balti language would be beamed from Radio Muzaffarabad. All India Radio, Leh did not broadcast any programme in Balti until 1975. The local authorities tried to restrict the people listening to such broadcast without any success. The content of the programmes in Balti from across the border is highly theocratic in nature consisting of recitations from the Holy Quran, commentaries on *hadith*, eulogies (*qa-asida*), dirges (*marsia*) religious discourses and the happening in and around the place across the border. Since the Balti ethinc affliation was much more stronger with the areas on the other side of the border and also because of their high degree of conformity to religion they follow the Baltis immensely liked the broadcasts from Radio Muzaffarabad.'

CHAPTER V

RELIGIOUS STRUCTURE AND CHANGE

A brief histrorical background of Buddhism in Kargil, and religious precepts of the Muslim of Kargil are furnished in the pages to follow in order to deal with the religious organisation in Kargil. Religious sepecialists and their respective functions have also been described in details . Cycle of festivals as practiced by the Muslims of Kargil and the nature of interaction between the Muslim and Buddhists figure in details.

Buddhism in Kargil :

Little is known about religious history of Kargil until 250 B.C. Prior to advent of Buddhism, Bonism, a Shamanistic devil charming nacromatic cult with devil dancing- largely intermixed with Buddhist externals prevailed". Subsequently, it was suppressed and its establishments were destroyed by the local rulers on their conversion to Buddhism from 7th century onward at the instigation of lamas, as it indulged freely in animal and human sacrifices and it is strictly frobidden by the lamaist hierarchy which holds the temporals rule in central and Western Tibet.

The credit of carrying the torch of Buddhism to Laddakh goes to the famous Buddhist monks Padmasambhava and Attisa.Padamasambhava, known in Laddakh as Rgyan Rinpoche, is supposed to be the founder of the first order of the first Buddhist monks or Lamas. The first monastery was built under his direction in 749 A.D. after the model of Nalanda. Padmasambhava is considered to be the reincarnation of the Dhyani Buddha Amitabha. Attisa (Deepankar) belonged to the famous Buddhist monastery of Vikramshila. He visited Laddakh in 1038 A.D. and founded once again a new order on a purer Buddhist model which he called *kah-dam,* 'Bound by the Order'. which afterwards became yellow cap seat (Gelukpa) . Attisa resorted to Celibacy and purged the rituals of much of its gosser devil worship.

Islam in Kargil :

The history of Islam in Kargil is irrevocably linked with the emergence and growth of the religion in the valley of Kashmir. Hence it will be worthwhile to look back on the advent and growth of Islam in Kashmir first and then turn attention of the reader to Kargil.

The foundation of Islam in Kashmir was laid by a famous Turkish saint Syed Sharafuddin alias Bulbul Shah whose name is irrevocably associated with Rinchen Bot. Rinchin was a restless soul due to his disenchantment with the then prevailing form of Buddhism. He wanted to embrace Hinduism and reportedly approached Kashmiri Brahmins for his intended conversion but he was not obliged by the Hindu clergy as he was not a Hindu by birth. One morning his slumber was broken by the sound of *azan*, his religious metamorphosis was complete. The caller for prayers was none else than Bulbul Shah himself. He approached Bulbul Shah and embraced Islam assuming the title of king Sadruddin. He built the first mosque in Srinagar and opened a free mess (*langar*) to feed the poor and named it after his preceptor 'Bulbul Langar'. Francke (1926:278) quotes a couplet of Bulbul Shah in which he describes the charecterietics of his new friend Rinchen. The couplet runs as follows :

Yar-a-man bahr-e-mahfil aarai
Shud tamashai har tamashai,
Roo-e-ookard dawa-e- Islam
Moo-e-oo-kard kufr araai,
Kufr-o-Islam raba chang aarad
Khud mar aan chang ra tamashai.

"My friend has become the ornament of assemblies. The observed of all observers, his face claims Islam and hair adorns paganism. He hold in his fist both paganism and Islam and his frst too is the cynosure of beholders".

During the reign of king Shahabuddin (1372 A.D.) Syed Ali Hamdani and his son Mir Mohammad Hamdani came to the valley with a train of 1,000 desciples for propagation of Islam in Kashmir. First they turned their attention towards the urban elite and then fanned out in the villages of Kashmir for proselytization. His arrival seems to have fixed the religion of Kashmir. Laddakh too could not remain immuned from the religious development in the valley. A ticklish poser which intrigued many scholars of western Laddakh is the religious composition of Kargil where, according to Census of India, 1961 the population of Shia Muslims is about 95.00 per cent.Census of India (1961, Vol IV, part VI No. 13) tries to furnish the following explanation to the above mentioned poser:

"In the past the Rajas of Skardo, Kiris, Totli, Kharmang etc. had a Parsian strain in them and they themselves claimed to be of Persian origin. Persia being the cradle of this seat of Mohammadanism, it was but natural that the country should in the long run, abide by a form of religion favoured by their rulers".

The above proportion holds good as long as Kargil is considered insulated from the valley of Kashmir, which is not a historical fact. Racorded history easily disapproves the above proposition.

During the reign of Sultan Hasan Shahmiri, Mir Shamsuddin Iraqi came to Kashmir in 1487 A.D. He was a Shia by faith and was sent by king Mirza Ismael of Khorasan as an ambassador to the court of the Kashmiri ruler Sultan Hasan Shah. First he converted a renowned sufi of his time Baba Ali Najjar of Hasnabad, then Malik Moose Raina, the Prime Minister of Hasan Shah, came to the Mir's fold. The former donated his estate at Zaddibal to Mir Iraqi which later became the fountainhead of Shiism not only for Kashmir but also for Laddakh and Baltistan. The biggest achievement of Mir Iraqi was to convert the martial Dardic tribe of Chaks to Shite faith. The Chaks came to the throne after the decay and subsequent fall of Shamiri dynasty and ruled Kashmir over forty years till the state was annexed by the Moghals. Mir Shamsuddin Iraqi is, therefore, the person who may be credited with laying the foundation of Shiism in Kashmir.

Since the majority of Muslim in Kashmir valley belong to the Sunni sect of Islam, the activities of Mir Iraqi were seen with suspicion and often displeased the rulers of Kashmir. Many times he was interned to Laddakh and Baltistan where he converted the Buddhist populations into Shiism. He established a network of *madarasahs* for teaching of Shiite theology. On his return to Srinagar, Mir Iraqi was supposedly killed by his adverseries and was buried at Zaddibal, near Srinagar. Mir Iraqi's son, Mir Danyai continued to stay at Skardo for propagation of Shiism. Later he was summoned by Mirza Haider Douglat Kashghari and was done to death.

Recorded historical evidence suggests that Shiism appears to have reached to Laddakh and Skardo from the valley of Kashmir.

Hashmatullah (Ibid:717) informs that Mir Shamsuddin Iraqi converted the first Muslim King of Kargil Habib Cho in 1500 A.D. Fauq (1963:12)tells about a considerable population of Shia Mosavi-al-Safavi Syeds in Kashmir who trace their descent from Mir Shamsuddin Iraqi who was a direct descendent of Imam Moosa Kazim (A.S.) in 26th ascending generation, hence the Mosavi Syeds trace their descent from the Imam.

The descendants of Mir Shamsuddin Iraqi are found at Kargil, Panikhar and Kartse. Some of the Shia Muslims in Kargil followed the teachings of one Syed Noor Bakhsh and call themselves as Noor Bakhshia. Census of India,1961 (Ibid.7) makes the follwing observation by quoting superindendent of Census Operation Report, 1911 (Vol.xx).

"In the sense of followers of Noorbakhsh, the whole of Baltistan once used to be Noor Bakhshi, but the term has a special significance now. Shamsuddin Iraqi is known to have done a great deal in promulgating the Shia doctorines in Kashmir, and he appears to have turned his efforts at the fomer place. He found the Musalmans of Kargil and Skardo as impervious to his doctorine, and contrived a compromise between Sunnism and Shiism, which is represented in the beliefs and practices of the present day Nur Bakhshis. In due course of time......most of these people became positively Shias.......They represent, thus the stage of transition between Sunnism and Shiism."

Mohibbul Hasan (1959) provides a deeper insight into the problem of Noorbakhshis.

"The founder of Noorbakhshis sect was Syed Mohammad Bin Abdullah who was born in 1393 A.D. in Mohistan. After completing his education he became a disciple of Khaja Ishaq Khatani. Khaja himself was a disciple of Syed Ali Hamdani. Khaja gave the title of Noorbakhsh (fountain of light) to Syed Mohammad Bin Abdullah. Abdullah declared himself to be the resunrected Imam Mehdi (A.S.). This immature claim attracted the wrath of Taimur's son and heir Shah Rukh who imprisioned Noorbakhsh thrice in order to compell the latter to forego his claims. Shah Rukh died in 1447 A.D. Consequently, Noorbakhsh was released and stayed at Rey where he died in 1464 at the age of 73 years.

"The Noorbakhsia movement had the orientation of sufiism and its propounder claimed to have seen God, and imbibed the teachings of Hazarat Ali (A.S.) through Imam Hazrat Jaffar-as-Sadiq (A.S.) . He preached abstention from worldly pleasures.

"The teachings of Syed Mohammad Nurbakhsh were influenced by Shiism. He believed that an Imam should be judicious, brave and descendant of Hazrat Ali (A.S.) and Fatima (S.A.)...........he always emphasized the fact that his objectives were to spread the religion of Hazrat Mohammad, and Twelve Imams. They observe Moharram and few of them wear black clothes as a sign of mourning". (Hasan quoted by Abbasi'»:437).

It is apparent from the above details that the Nurbakhshia movement was nearest to Shiite Ethna-e-ashari faith. Hence the tenets of Nurbakhshia sect should be considered in cotents and spirits only as a sub sect of the former and not a separate sect of Islam as the differences between the Shiite faith and Nurbakhshia philosophy are narrow and subtle.

The Nurbakhsi regulate their day to day life under the guidance of Nurbakhsh whereas the Shias Ethna-e-ashari do not believe in a dead Imam. They believe that their 12th Imam is still alive but is in hiding. The Shias therefore are governed by his deputies (*mujtahid*). Hence it is obligatory for each Shia individual to follow a living mujtahid (*taq-leed*).

Nurbakhshis rever one of the Prophet Mohammads' wife wheraas the Shias condemn her for her animosity against Hazart Ali (A.S.).

The Shia use the pharase *haiya-ala-Khairul amal'* in call for prayers whereas the Nurbakhsis use the term *'haiva ala Khairul bashar:'*

Notwithstanding the differences between the two schools of thoughts, both believe in similar ablutions, prayers and the holy book Quran.

The Nurbakhshi tenets are coded in "Kitab-e-ahwat" which is now untraccable hence the Nurbakhsia refer to the Shia priests for guidance. Inter marriages between the two groups are also common in Kargil.

RELIGIOUS PRECEPTS

Islam is the word generally used by the Muslims of Kargil for the religion they follow. The term implies submission and recognition to the will of God in all matters of faith and duty.

A tree is composed of roots and its various branches. If Islam is a tree its tenets may be divided into roots (*usool-e-din*) and branches (*fru-e-din*)

Usool-e-din : The Roots of Religion

I Tawheed : Ultimate unity or Oneness of God.

II Adl : Ultimate justice of God.

III Naboowat : (Prophethood)God has sent one hundred and twenty four thousand Prophets for guidance of His people. Adam being the first and Mohammad being the last Prophet of God.

IV Imamat : After termination of Prophethood, Imams were assigned by Allah to carry further the massage of the Prophet Mohammad. In all there are 12 Imams for the guidance of the people . Their names, relationship with the Prophet Mohammad, the respective years of their birth and death and their mode of death are furnished in the following table:

Sl no.	Name of Imam	Relationship with the Prophet Mohammad	Year of birth (A. D.)	Year of death (A.D.)	Mode of death	Place of burial
1.	Ali Ibn-e-Abi Talib	Fa Br S and Da H	598	661	Assassinated	Najaf Ashraf
2.	Hasan Ibn-e-Ali	Da So (S/o Ali)	623 or 625	670	Poisoned to death	Jannatul-Baqi (Medina)
3.	Hussain Ibn-e-Ali	(Da SO) S/o of Ali	626	680	Assasinated	Karbala-e Maulla (Iraq)
4.	Ali Ibnul Hussain (Zainul Abedin)	(Da So So) S/o of Hussain	658	716	Poisoned to death by Walid bin Abdul Malik Marwan	Jannat-ul-Baqi Medine
5.	Mohammad-al-Baquir	(Da So So So) S/o of Ali Ibnul Hussain	677	739	Piosoned to death by Hisham bin Abdul Malik	-do-
6.	Jaffar-as- Sadiq	S/o of Mohammad Baqir	704	769	Poisoned to death by Mansour Dawa--neequ, the Abbaside	-do-
7.	Moosa-al-Kazim	S/o of Jaffar-as - Sadiq	749	804	Poisoned to death by Harm	Kazma-ainra
8.	Ali Raza	S/o of Moosa Kazim		765	818 Poisoned to death by Mamoon, the Abbaside Caliph	Meshhac Iran
9.	Mohammad Taqi	S/o of Ali Raza	811	841	Poisoned to death by Mutasin, the Abbaside	Kazmain Iraq
10.	Ali Naqi	S/o of Moham mad and Taqi	833	875	Poisoned to death by Mutasin, the Abbaside	Samarra Iraq
11.	Hasan Askari	S/o of Ali Naqi	853	881	Poisoned to death by Mohammad the Abbaside ruler	
12.	Mohammad-al Mahdi	S/o of Hassan Askari	869	---	Believed to be alive, in hiding	

V Qiamat : There will be a day when everything will perish from the face of earth except God, who will reanimate the dead enabling them to face the judgement for their virtues and misdeeds. God will send the virtuous to Paradise and evildoers to Hell for all eternity .

Sunnis and Shias :

Allah directs all men and women to the path of righteousness. The path is shown to the people by his Prophets. Mohammad, the last Prophet, was bestowed with the Holy Quran, a book calling men to believe in the Unity of God. Soon after Mohammad died, the Muslims found themselves divided in two groups on the question of succession. Sunnis, a term generally applied to a large section of Muslims population, acknowledged Abu Bakr as first caliph and the immediate successor of prophet Mohammad by a consensus. The followeres of Ali, who were latter referred as Shias considered him to be the immediate successor and heir of Prophet Mohammad. Ali being the first cousin of the Prophet and the husband of his dauhgter Fatima, was the closest among the kin of the Prophet. The Shias therefore rejected Abu Bakr, who happened to be companion and father-in law-of the prophet Mohammad as his immediate successor. They treated the first true Caliphs Abu Bakar, Umar and Usman, as usurpers (Huges, 1885/572). Ummaiyad (661-749 A.D.), Abbasits (750-1258) and Ottoman (1299- 1876) were successive dynasties of the Caliphs who ruled over the temporal and religious world of Islam. The Shias on the other hand, believe and follow in a straight line of descent as shown in the table mentioned above. After the disappearance of the 12th Imam in the year 869 A.D. the Shias follow mujtahids, 'enlightened doctors' who interprete and explain explicitly the Divine orders, rules and regulation from the denotations, the cannotations, and the implications contained in Quran and the authentic sayings of the Prophet Mohammad and Twelve Imams. They can not use their discretion in the findings, parallel to the Quran and tradition (*hadith*) but only their sound reasoning in understanding Quran *hadithand sunnat.*

This capability is inculcated to the priests in selected *madarasahs* which are mostly situated in Iraq and Iran where internees from all over the world seek the highest degree of religious learning (*ijtihad*). Such accomplished priests can be easily recognised by their turban (black for Syeds and white for non-Syeds). The role of *mujtahids* in the life cycle of the Shias of Kargil will be discussed later in this report.

Branches of Religion (Furo-e din) :

A tree can not survive without its roots and branches, similarly, without an unqualified belief in the tenets described above one can not claim to be a devout muslim and a Shia. Islam has a number of branches (*fro-e-din*) through which the faith of an individual thrives. the brancehs areas stated below :

1. Namaz
2. Roza
3. Hajj
4. Zakaat
5. Khums
6. Jehad

Namaz is incumbent upon every man and woman who has attained maturity and is of same mind to pray five times in a day. The prayers are compulsory (*wajib*) which must be performed regularly even if a person is indisposed or travelling from one place to another. The five daily prayers performed by the Muslims of Kargil in particular and Muslims in general are as follows:

Namaz-e-fajr :

Fajr falls under the category of morning prayers and is performed 80 minutes before the sun rise. *Namaz-e-Zohar* is a mid day prayers which is performed when sun starts coming down from its peak but before sun set. *Namaz-e-asr* is performed any time after Zohar prayers but before sun set. *Namaz-e-maghrib* Maghrib prayers are performed 8 to 15 minutes after sun-set. *Namaz-e-isha* : Isha prayers are performed after Meghrib but before midnight.

Precondition for Observance of Namaz Ablutions :

There are pre-conditions for performance of each of above mentioned prayers viz., bodily cleanliness and ritual purity. The believer must make it sure that his body, cloths and place of prayer are clean (*paak*). Before performing prayers, ritual ablution (*wazu*) is essential. Ablution may be carried out by water. If later is not available or it is likely to cause harm to the health of the believer, in that case dry sand or clay may be used in lieu of water (*taimum*).

Baths :

Purificatory baths (*ghusl*) are obligatory in the following conditions :

(a) Emission of semen or coition (*janabat*)

(b) Bathing of a dead body before burial (*ghusl-e-maiyat*)

(c) If some one touches a dead body before the purificatory bath is carried out on the dead body, he or she will have to take a bath (*ghusl-e-mas-e-maiyat*).

(d) After discharge of menstrual blood (*ghusl-e-istahaza*)

(e) After discharge followed by parturition (*ghusl-e-nifaas*)

Mass prayers in a mosque bring more credit than prayers performed individually at home. An assembly of prayers is constituted by at least two persons one who leads the prayers (Imam) and one who performs the prayers under the guidance of the *Imam* (*mamoon*). In Friday prayers, the congregation must be composed of at least 5 persons.

Those who are sick, invalid or rendered unfit to perform prayers regularly enjoy the following concessions in observance of prayers :

I. If a person can not stand erect,he/she should stand with a support.

II. If a person cannot stand even with a support he/she may sit on a chair and use a table for prostration (*sajda*).

III. If a person is unable to sit on a chair he/she must lie on his/her right side facing west (in direction of Mecca).

IV. If this is also not possible, then he/she should lie down facing west.

It has already been mentioned that each village in Kargil contains at least one or more than one mosques for performance of daily prayers. Mosques are built by voluntary contributions made by the villagers themselves. Labour is given free.

Before commencement of prayers, the caller (*muazzin*) calls for the prayers (*azzan*) to which people respond quickly and run towards the mosque.After taking ablutions they stand in rows facing west (*qibla*). After prayers are over,people shake hands and embrace each other. Women pray at home. Children of pre- puberty age are exempted from regular prayers but if they do so the credit goes to the parents.

Muslim society in Kargil has not evolved any sanctions against those who do not perform prayers. Such non-conformists will be answerable to Allah on the last day of Judgement (Qiamat).

Unlike other parts of Kashmir valley where mosques are used as a political platform, they are relatively free in Kargil from ploitical activities. Even Moharram congregations, religious in content and spirit, are usually performed in a separate building locally referred as *matamsara*.

Rozah :

Thirty days of fasting are obligatory for all men and women in the month of Ramzan, the ninth month of the Islamic Calender. The sick, pregnant ladies, children and infirm are exempted from observance of fasting. Travellers on journey for more than 3 days are also exempted from fasting during the duration of journey .

The timings for beginning and the end of the fast are printed and distributed to the people free of cost. The fast usually starts in early hours of the morning with *sahr* i.e. morning breakfast and is broken after the sunset when the people assemble in the village mosque, perform *namaz* and break the fast *(iftar)* initially with a piece of salt or a piece of earth from Karbala (*khak-e-shifa*) and a glass of water. Cooked food or snacks are sent to the mosque by various households of the village. The eatables are pooled and distributed to all those present in the mosques at the time of *iftar* (breaking fast).

Hajj :

Hajj literally means "setting out" or "tending towards". The pilgrimage to Mecca becomes obligatory on one who possesses enough to meet the expenses of journey as well as for the maintenance of the remaining members of the family left behind. A pilgrim should redress all the wrongs done by him, pay all the outstanding debts before setting out for the Hajj pilgrimage. He must not borrow in order to meet Hajj expenses. Those who return after pilgrimage are called as Alhaj or Haji. In Kargil however there is a slight difference in the cannotation of the term '*haji*' .This title is conferred on those who return not necessarily from a pilgrimage in Mecca but go to visit the shrines of various Imams and close kin and companions of the Prophet Mohammed and Imam situated in Iraq ,Iran and Syria. The financial restrictions imposed on Haj pilgrim are not applicable in this case.

Zakaat :

Zakaat is a levy payable at the rate of 40th part of one's movable property items like gold and silver ornaments, coins, wheat, barley and cattle. The amount thus collected goes to deserving individuals and Islamic *madarasahs.*

Khums :

Khums is a cess levied at the rate of one fifth part of the total savings at the year and after deducting all legitimate expenses from the earning of that particular year. The *Khums* levy is divided into two parts.

(a) Mal-e-Imam

(b) Mal-e-Sadat

Mal-e-Imam is divided into two equal halves. One half goes to the deputies of the Imam, viz., *Mujtahid* priests and the second half is spent for the maintenance of Islamic *madarasah.*

Half portion of mal-e-sadet goes to the Saiyids who are the direct descendants of the Prophet Mohammad and the other half is donated to Islamic *madarasah.*

Three Syed families in Hardas who serve this and other surrounding villages do not own any land. Their maintenance largely depends on *mal-e-saadat* portion of the *Khums* levy. They receive their due share both in cash and in kind which includes dry apricots, cattle, fuel wood or timber, cattle, mutton on festival occasions when sacrifices are performed in the village after harvest and poultry birds.

Jehad :

Jehad literally means an affort' or a 'striving'against unbelievers in the mission of Prophet Mohammad. Striving can be of various kinds and in different ways which includes a war when it is the only alternative to defend the faith and the faithful.

RELIGIOUS FUNCTIONERIES /SCARED SPECIALISTS

Day to day life of an individual in Kargil is supervised by three categories of clergy, viz. Agha, Sheikh and Akhun. They imbibe Islamic learning in Middle East but the Akhun receive their training in the *madarsahs* of Kargil. A *madarsah* named Madarsa-e- Islamiya at Kargil imparts advance training in Shia theology. Each category of religious functioneries and their functions will be described below :

Priesthood is an achieved social identity which any one can acquire depending on his inclination and resources. Women are barred from being priests though their is no religious instruction. A Saiyed priest (*mujtahid*) is known as Agha in Kargil whereas an ordinary Syed is usually refered as Shah. By virtue of their kinship ties with the Prophet Mohammad (S.A.) the Saiyied enjoy highest place in the local hierarchy. A mujtahid priest is distinct in his apparel and mannerism. He wears a black (in case of Syeds) or white (if non- Syed) headgear (*amama*) and a usually a black tunic coming down to the feet. He is usually a sober person who avoids interactions with the people publicly excepting when he leads a prayer or delivers a sermon. Most of his time is spent in meditation and imparting religious knowledge to his pupil,and guiding the people in the performance of various life cyle rituals. Soon after a child is born, the Agha is called to recite verses from Holy Quran in the ears of the infant. He recites verses and blesses a male child in event of latter's circumcission (*khatna*) ceremony. No marriage is possible without recitation of prescribed verses and the prior approval of the couple for marriage (*nikah*). Invariably the Agha is called for recitation of nikah verses known as segha. During a funeral ceremony of a male member he supervises all the funerary rites.

In Hardas, a boy, named Sultan Ahmad, was killed by a mine blast. While giving purificatory bath to the dead body (*gusl-e-maiyat*) a controversy came up. A body dismembered so much that the flesh has come out of the bones is not given a wet bath (*ghusl*) but a dry bath (*taimum*). In the present case, the boy had lost one leg below the thigh pieces of which got scattered in a wide area due to impact of explosion, hence the leg could not be restored. There was also a big gaping hole in the chest. Some elders prescribed *taimum* instead of *ghusl*. The Agha was consulted. He came, inspected the body and consulted books. Ultimately he gave the ruling that excepting leg portion, the body was intact with the flesh, hence *ghusl-e-maiyat* could be given to the dead body.

The Aghas lead a life of virtual seclusion, though socially they are the part of the village population by marrying with non- Syeds. The rule of endogamy does not operate among the Muslims of Kargil. His relative seclusion is a direct outcome of his non- participation in secular and economic activities of the villages.

It has been said earlier that Aghas do not own land in Hardas. They eke out their livelihood by receiving *Khums*, presentation during festivals, marriages and other life cycle rituals and by teaching pupil. There is no prescribed fee for teaching children but gifts and presentation are acceptable to them. Making presentation to a Saiyed in general and to a Saiyed priest in particular brings merit (*sawab*) to the people.

Sheikhs :

Non-Saiyed Mujtahids are known as Sheikhs who are next to Agha priests in the social hierarchy of a village. A Sheikh wears a white headgear he, being the autocthone is relatively more active participants in the secular and economic activities of the respective kingroups. Sheikh Hasan of Hardas, an accomplished *mujtahid* performed supervisory roles in the family economy as the head to the household. When apricots were sun-dried and ready for sale he would go to Kargil with labourers carrying the bags full of the commodity for selling. Once in a while he used to go to Sringar for making bulk purchases of butter, tea,salt, biscuits, clothes and spices as the Zoji pass remains closed for 5 months to traffic during winters. In his spare time he helped his brothers to carry out necessary repairs in the house. He also adjudicated small disputes relating to families or land in accordance with the provisions of *Shara.* One of the Sheikhs in Hardas is a teacher in Government School at Kargil.

Akhun :

Akhun is priest-cum-medicineman, almost a counterpart of *amchi* found among the Buddhists. His position in the priestly group is not as high as a Sheikh or an Agha. Nevertheless, he enjoys a very high reputation in the village. The Akhun of Hardas was the village postmaster. Akhun Taqi of Wakha successfully filled the void caused by the indifferent health of Sheikh Moosa, priest of the village. An Akhun possessed a deep knowledge of supernatural spirits, and demons (ilm-e-ramal). On occasions, he acted as a shaman and cured a patient by invoking the asistance of a *djinn,* who are, according to Islamic philosophy, of a different species members of which look like men but they may disguise themselves in the form of cats, dogs and lions etc. An Akhun remembers by heart a number of incantations and prayers (*dua*) which have therapeutic powers. Some of these prayers are effective to control certain calamities like termors, storms, rains and epidemics. These prayers are written on small piece of paper as charms and are encased in silver casket to be worn either as a necklace or a bracelet. In absence of a metallic container the charms are sewn in a waxed cloth. Numerology is also resorted to cause good effect on the health of a patient. Each Arabic alphabet is allotted a number ranging from 1 to 1000. The permutation and combination of these compose a prayer. 786 for example, oannotes a famous Muslim prayer. Bismillah' which is uttered before starting any work. The word literally mean" I beg in with the name of Allah". The Akhun by his knowledge about prayers cures the ailments by giving charms (*ta:viz*) according to the nature of illness. The charms belong to the following categories:

(a) Thangmi ta : viz : The charm is soaked in water to cure patient suffering from body and toothache.

(b) Hardoqpi ta:viz: It is burnt and the ashes are applied to cure opthalmic disorders.

(c) Taapti ta:viz: The charm is worn either as a necklace or an armlet for curing mental disorders.

Religious Performances :

It has been said earlier that 95 per cent population of Kargil belong to Shia Ethna-e-ashari sub-sect of Islam. The first month according to Islamic calender is Moharram. Moharram heralds nine weeks of mourning devoted mainly to the memory of tragic battle of Karbala between the third Imam Hussain Ibn-e-Ali, his close kin and companions and the armies of Yazid, the then Caliph. The issues involved in the battle are well known hence need no repetition. Here description will be confined to various Moharram rituals performed by the Baltis of Kargil. Congregations start from 1st Moharram in the afternoon when people assemble in *matamsara* after attending routine daily chores.

A congregation (*majlis*) starts with recitation of dirges (*marsia-Khaan*) . It is followed with the arrival of priest for delivery of a sermon. The priest sits on a pulpit (*mimbar-e-Rasool*), a replica of one on which the Prophet used to sit and deliver sermons. The sermon begins with recitation of Koranic verses, their interpretations and applicability in day to day life of an individual in the way they were adapted by Prophet Mohammad, various Imams and their close kin in their daily life.This involves bringing the individual merits of the holy men in the limelight in order to show how best one can emulate the examples of these exalted heroes. The speaker concludes his address with the narration of sufferings and hardships faced by Imam Hussain, his relatives and associates. The audience react to the narration by an expression of intense emotion : loudly crying and beating their breast. The crescendo dies down slowly as the priest comes down from the pulpit. The discourse is followed with lamentations (*nauha khani*) amidst flagelating of breast (*barangghuduns*). This being over,the priests prays for the well being of the community (*dua-e-khair*). Such congregations (*majlis*) bring all other activities in the village to a total stand still. The women folk sit behind carved wooden screens but the young girls of 5 to 6 years sit with their male elders in the central hall of *matamsara*.

The following table furnishes a chronological sequence of main Moharram rituals which start from appearance of the moon and last for next ten days.

Days of Moharram	Name of the martyr commemorated	Related activities
1st Moharram	All martyrs	A black flag is hoisted on matamsara signifying the beginning of Moharram mournings. Women break their bangles in the shrine, abstain from putting on jewellery and coloured clothes, combing hair, applying oil to their heads.
2nd Moharram	-	The priest addresses a congregation *(majlis)* in the matamsara narrating the course of journey followed by Imam Hussian and his carvan or 72 individuals from Medina to Mecca and onward to Karbala.
3rd Moharram	-	Congregation is held. The Sheikh narrates about the preparation regarding establishment of camp by Imam Hussain on the banks of the Euphrates river.
4th Moharram	Hazrat Muslim bin Aqeel	A cousin of Imam Hussain Hazrat Aqeel was invited by the residents of Koofa where he and his two sons were treacherously killed by the adversaries of Imam Hussain. His sufferings are narrated by the priest in the shrine.
5th Moharram	Sons of Muslim-bin-Aqeel	The day is commemrated to the memory of two sons of Hazrat Aqeel who were also assassinated with their father.
6th Moharram	Hazarat Ali Akbar son of Imam Husain	The day is consecrated to the memory of the youthful son of Imam Hussan who gave his life at the early age of 18 years to defend the cause of his father.
7th Moharram	Hazrat Qasin son of Imam Hasan, the elder brother of Imam Hussain	A congregation is held in the memory of a young boy who was married a couple of days earlier but left his wedlock to give his life for the cause of Imam Hussain at the age of 14 years.

8th Moharram	Hazrat Ali Asghar, son of Imam Hussain	The narration of this infant son of Imam Husain draws loudest lamentations as the priest describes the restive state of a six month old child who was denied water since 7th of Moharram. On the last day of battles Imam Hussain begged for a few drops of water for the infant who was almost dying of thirst. The enemy replied his request with an arrow which pierced the throat of the child. The child died instaneoulsy. Imam Husian buried him in the desert sand. After the narration comes to an end, a replica of the cradle used by the infant is taken round the matamsara abemidst loud cries by the people present in the congregation who sceramble to touch the cradle.
9th Moharram	Hazrat Abbas brother of Imam Husain	Hazarat Abbas, the standard bearer of the small army of Imam Hussain was one of the most awesome, daring and brave soldiers of Imam Hussain's army when he sought permission to offer his life for the cause. Imam Hussain asked him to bring water from Euphrate canal which was heavily guarded by the enemy lest water reaches to the camp of Imam Hussain. Hazrat Abbas surged forward towards the canal and reached on its banks breaking the stiff enemy resistence. He filled his goat-skin bag and started returning towards his camp.The enemy encircled him but he fought bravely and tried hard to break the circle, got both of his hands severed in the process and ultimately succumbed to injuries. In the night all villagers assemble in *matamsara* and pass the night in listening religious discourses, reciting dirges and lamentation till the dawn of 10th Moharram. It is considered uncouth to sleep in the night that is know as *shab-e-aashoora.*
10th Moharram	Imam Hussain	The day, known as *ashoor* starts with morning prayers (*namaz*). After prayers,a congregation (*majlis*) is held in *matamsara* which is addressed by a priest. After *majlis* people disperse for a couple of hours and reassemble for another congregation. Before sermon starts, a replica of the standard of Imam Hussin *(alam)* is brought in procession to the village matamsara from nearby villages. The villagers now carry

		their own *alam* in a procession and go to other villages. All villagers observe a day's fast on this day irrespecitve of age and sex. Infants, children, pregnant women, sick and infirm are exempted form fasting. Other activites in the village come to a complete halt. Men and women pass their time either in listening congregation or observing prayers. The fast is broken late in afternoon.
13th Moharram	*Martyrs* of *Karbala* (Irbazdus)	The day is passed in *majilis* reciting dirges and lamentations. The congregation begins in the afternoon and continues foran hour.or so. All Moharram performances come to end with *Irbazdus* but the period of mourning however continues.

Nishuniz :

Nishuniz falls on the 20th day of Safar, the second month of Islamic calendar. The day falls on the 40th day after the battle of Karbala and thus the day is devoted to the martyrs of Karbala. The learned elite of the village refer the day as *arbaeen*. This day is commemorated in the memory of the remaining members mainly consisting of widows and children, of Imam Husian's carvan which returned to Medina after the battle and held an assembly mourning the dead. The villagers of Kargil commemorate the event by reciting dirges and lamentations.

Death Anniversary of Prophet Mohammad :

The death anniversary of Prophet Mohammad is observed on 28th of Safar by the villagers making offerings and supplications.

Id-e-Baqr :

Moharram observances come to an end in the next month Rabiul awwal. The mourning is replaced by rejoicings. On 9th Rabiulawwal Id-e-Baqr is celebrated. People rejoice on the death of Umar-bin-saad, the commander of Yazid's forces who killed Imam Husain, his relatives and close companions. The women put on bangles and other ornaments, they wear gaudy and colourful clothes. Special food is cooked and offered to guests in each house of the village. The sense of rejoicings is expressed by the people by embracing each other.In the night an assembly is held in which qualities of Imams are narrated in verses (*qa:sida*). Such eulogies are written in Balti language.

Birthday of the Prophet Mohammad :

The brith anniversery of the Prophet falls on 17th of Rabi-ul- awwal. The day is passed in making offerings to the departed soul of the Prophet and other members of his family (*nazar*) *Qa : sida* are recited in the evening congregation.

Death Anniversary of Fatima Zahra :

On jamadi-ul-awwal, the fifth month of Islamic calender, the death anniversary of Janab-e-Fatima (S.A.) the daughter of Prophet Mohammad and also the mother of Imam Hasan and Imam Hussain, is observed. A majlis is held in the village *matamsara* in which women participate actively. Refreshment (*tabarruk*) in the form of tea or condiments is distributed after the congregation.

Birth Anniversary of Janab-e-Fatima :

The birth anniversary of Janab-e-Fatime Zahra (S.A.) falls on the 20th day of Jama-d-ul sahi, the sixth month of Islamic calender. Wearing the new clothes the villagers visit their relatives in their own or the adjoining villages. The guests are entertained with tea. Public congregations (*mahfil*) are held in the night in which *qa : sidas* are recited.

Birth Anniversary of Hazrart Ali :

The birthday of Hazrat Ali falls on 13th of Rajab, the seventh month of Islamic calender. In Kargil this day is passed amidst rejoicings (*eid*). People put on their best clothes and special food is cooked and offered to the guests in each house of the village.

Villagers pass the evening in a congregation in which the village priest delivers a sermon eulogizing the individual merits and qualities of Hazrat Ali (A.S.) and other members of his family (*ahl-e-baiit*).

Id-e-ba: Sat :

On 27th of Rajab, Prophet Mohammad was ordained as a Prophet of God. The festival commemorates the day on which Mohammad bil Abdullah was ordained as the last Prophet of God. The day falls on 27th of Rajab, the seventh month of the Muslim calender.

Birth Anniversary of Imam Husain :

The birth anniversary of Imam Husain falls on 3rd day of Sha: ban, the eighth month of Islamic calender. Like other birth anniversaries, the people rejoice the event by attending a congregation in the village *matamsara*.

Shab-e-bara:at :

The 14th day of Sha:ban is a day of rejoicing as the last living Imam-al-Mahdi (A.S,)was born on this day. People illuminate their houses with candles, offerings are made to the Imam and the night is passed in prayers.

Ramza:n-ul-Mubarik :

Ramza:n, the ninth month of Islamic calender is considered holy. It is obligatory on the part of every adult Muslim to observe fast on all days of month from dawn to dusk (roza/som). Early in morning a batch of men move from house to house invoking the people to observe the fast. The fast is broken in the late evening after performance of evening prayers by eating first a piece of clay brought from Karbala (*Khak-e-Shifa*) and salt. This is followed by other eatables. The fast is broken either in the mosque or at different houses of the village. Those who observe fast are invited by co-villagers for a fast-breaking feast (*Roza Shikani* or *iftaar*).

Shab-e-qadr :

On 19th Ramaza:n, the Holy Quran descended on Prophet Mohammad (A.S.). On this night as assasin attacked Hazrat Ali while he was observing prayers in a mosque. The people go to *matamsara*, for listening sermons eulogising the individual qualities of Hazrat Ali. This and successive two nights are passed in prayers and supplication. The death of Hazart Ali is mourned on 21st of Ramza:n.

Id-ul-fitr:

Id-ul-fitr heralds the end of the month of fasting as it falls on the first of Shawwal; the tenth month of Islamic calender. In the morning the entire male population and young girls assemble in the village mosque for special id prayers (*namaz-e-id*). The prayer is led by the Sheikh. After prayers are over, each head of the household in the village gives *fitra*or *zakat-e-badni* in the hands of the *mujtahid* at the rate of 3kgs. of food grains (staple) per members of the family or money equal to the prescribed quantity of the food grains. This money is spent to maintain the deserving members of the community like, beggars, students with no source of income and orphans. After prayers people return to their houses. Special dishes, viz., sweets (*halwa*) mutton and fried rice seasoned with mutton (*biryani*) are cooked. The evening is spent in meeting close relatives.

Id-e-qurban :

Id-e-qurban falls on 10th day of Zilhijj, the 12th month of Islamic calender. The festival is commemorated in the memory of great sacrifice offered to Allah by Prophet Abraham who agreed to sacrifice his own son,

Ismail in order to obey the command of Allah. Allah commanded the faithful Prophet to slaughter his only son in His name. The Prophet performed the act faithfully obeying the command of his Creator. By miracle his son was standing at a distance unharmed. A sheep instead was lying in a pool of blood. Allah was satisfied by the submission of the Prophet Abraham.

To commemorate the above event the villagers of Kargil observe *id-e-qurban* by saying prayers and sacrificing a sheep or goat in the name of Allah. The mutton is distributed among the relatives and co-villagers.

Eid-e-Ghadir :

On this day according to the informants Prophet Mohammad proclaimed Ali as his successor and immediate heir at a place known as *Ghadir-e-Khum* while he was returning after performance of Hajj at Mecca. The *eid* is celebrated on 18th day of Zilhijja.

In the evening the Sheikh delivers a sermon enumerating and eulogising the individual merits (*seerat*) of Prophet Mohammad and his cousin Hazrat Ali. Like all other festivals people put on their best clothes, women apply myrtle (*hinna*) paste on their hands which turns them red, scents and perfumes are sprinkled liberally on one's own self and on the bodies of guests and visitors. Special food is cooked.

It may be observed that ritual performances in Kargil may be divided in two broad categories viz. festive performances and mournful performances. Most of ritual performances in Kargil revolve round the Prophets, Fatima (S.A.) and 12 Imams. Their birth anniversaries and special deeds bring cheers and rejoicings to the people whereas their deaths cause mournings expressed through intense emotional expression ranging from wailing, crying, breast beating and inflicting wounds on parson with sharp edged weapons to introvert meditation. These events do not confine only to the realm of religion but extend beyond becoming a part and parcel of all the life cycle rituals, social and economic organisations.

The Changing Scene :

It has already been observed that the people of Kargil were Buddhists till the arrival of Mir Shamsuddin Iraqi in Baltistan. MIor converted the Buddhists of Baltistan and Kargil into Shiism but soon the undercurrents of Buddhism reemerged in the society. The people of Kargil evolved an intricate balance between their old faith Buddhism and new faith Islam. This equilibrium remained undisturbed and intact till 1947. After emergence of a theocratic sovereign state close to the borders of Kargil a new wave of Islamic resurgence swept Kargil. The expanding network of communications funnelled in cash earning to Kargil, which was invested in strengthening and cementing somewhat brittle Islamic form of society. Young village lads from all corners of Kargil found their way to Islamic *madarasas* in Iraq and Iran for acquiring religious learning. These novices returned to their villages as full fledged *mujtahid* priests armed with the capablities to guide the people to the path of righteousness. The life style of the people of Kargil considerably changed and their dependence on religion increased. They became more and more introvert fatalists. The sound of music and hillarity of horse-polo (*chaugan*) became a past story. Marriages were stripped of much of their traditional music and fanfair. The traditional musicians cases of the Dom had to change their ethic identity and occupational specialisation and they became artisans (*Mistri*). The world view matured under theocratic dogmatism resisted the penetration of sacular and democratic value in Kargil. This also resulted into declining social interaction of the people of Kargil with their Buddhists and Kashmiri (*kache-pa*) neighbours.

The trend now is changing again . The people are increasingly becoming responsive to modern medicines and secular education. Muslim girls, though of young age, have started going to schools where co-education is in vogue. The opening of Laddakh to foreign tourists has brought about a sea change in the attitude of the people of Kargil- the influence of the priests as a force of political decision making also seems to be on a decline.

CHAPTER VI

POLITICAL STRUCTURE AND CHANGE

Political History of Kargil :

The earliest settlers of the area are supposed to be the Mons who were displaced by Dards and subsequently the Dards were displaced by the Mongols who established their fiefs in Kargil. Some of the main rulers of Kargil were the rulers of Suru, Kartse, Chiktan, Wakha, Gilgit, Chiktan and Kharmang.

The Gazetteer of Kashmir and Laddakh (534) describes the former Governments as a "mild despotism, under the ruler who bore the title Gyalpo"(p.534).

The conduct of affairs was generally entrusted to the minister or Kahlon. His power was apparently absolute, but was really curbed by the wide spread authority of the monastic establishments and by the partial independence of the petty *gyalpos* and district *Kahlons*. His office was almost heriditary. Many of the nobility were petty chiefs of the valleys which had once been independent. There was a *gyalpo* in Nubra Zanskar and Pashkyum, etc. Among the Government officers, the deputy *Kohlon* was called as *Kahlon rigesn* or *nono-kahlon* : The other officers were the *lonpos* : or governors of towns, and *Kharpons,* or commanders in chief, the *chagsot* or treasure, the *shogaur-chagsot* or head collector of taxes *Shakspon* or chief justice, the *Khrunpons* or magistrates, *Kaka-tadsi* or master of the horse, and *chagsi-gopa* or kotwal.

The inferior officers were the *mipons* or *gopas* the headman of the villages, and the *shogumpa,* or provincial collectors of taxes and customs.

The administration of justice was formerly patriarchal, assembly of five or seven elders was called by the district *gyalpo* or *Kahlon,* or by the village *gopa* to decide cases. The punishments were stripes, fines and imprisonment: in extreme cases banishment or death. Death was seldom awarded and still more rarely carried out. Criminals were either crucified or thrown into streams bound hand and foot, and weighted with stones. Banishment, or rather ignonimous expulsion from society, preceded by stripes and branding was the usual punishment for murder. For child murder a women was sentenced to the loss of one hand in addition to the above expulsion. (.537).

Vexed by the repeated attacks of Baltis and Sokpas, a Mogul tribe, the *Gyalpos* called for the aid of the Goverment of Kashmir who defeated the Sokpas and drove them out of the country. From this time the *Gyalpos* of Laddakh began to pay tributes to the Governors of Kashmir.

In 1834 Gulab Singh of Jammu invaded Laddakh under the command of Wazir Zorawar Singh, who built a fort at Suru and advanced futher to Pashkyum and was opposed by the Laddakhis at Pashkyum bridge. Pashkyum was now abandoned and the chief fled to the fort of Sod. The Dogras took the fort and *Gyalpo* and about six hundred Laddakhis were taken prisoners. Since then Laddakh remained under the Dogra of Jammu till the whole state of Jammu and Kashmir was merged with Republic of India.

The Contemporary Political Set Up :

Gopa is the unit of political control in a village and it is headed by a *numbardar* whose office is hereditary in character. The numbardar during the *Shakshi Raaj* was responsible for collection of revenue on the *panjotra* basis, i.e., keeping one fifth of the total revenue collection as his remuneration and deposit the remaining amount in the treasury in Kargil. He was also repsonsible for supplying *ress* (forced labour to Goverment functionaries). The mode of collecting *ress* was by rotation. The numbardar, was, however, exempted from forced labour. He was also responsible for arranging pack animals for the Government. Besides revenue collection, procuring labour supply, and supply of pack animals, the numbardar was also responsible for maintaining a register of births and deaths and to inform police in case of an eventuality in the village.

In case a hereditary *numbardar* was not available the villagers would select an influential and educated person of their choice. The Wazir-e-Wazarat would then issue a *sanad* (letter of appointment) to the person selected by the villagers. Thereafter, Tehsildar would issue the letter of appointment on the behalf of Deputy Commissioner.

Now, lands which fetch a revenue of Rs. 9.00 or less have been exempted from revenue collection. Since the size of landholdings are very small, most of the villagers, have, thus been exempted form paying revenue to the *numbardar.* The new Land Reform Act, thus, eroded the authority of a *numbardar* considerably besides his income was also adversely affected. Since the arrival of armed forces in the area for defence of border, army *numbardars* were selected in border villages on a fixed salary. The functions of army *numbardars* are the same as of former *numbardars* : supplying wage labourers and pack animals to Brigade office, help army in war efforts by keeping the routes open, otherwise blocked by land slides and snow. The army *numbardar* sends the labourers by rotation. His decision in the selection of labourers is considered by other villagers as final. The category of the people exempted from army labour are elderly persons, women and children; the Sheikhs and Akhuns and the numbardar himself.

Hasan was the traditional numbardar of Hardas village but he was found ineffective for the villagers. Subsequently a burly Haji Mehdi in his late fifties was selected by Brigade office as Army numbardar. Haji Mehdi, worked very hard to refurnish the image of the village and established a good rapport with the local Brigade.

Male Khan (Mohammad Ali Khan) was the traditional and hereditary *numbardar* of Wakha. Since Wakha is not a border village, the village did not possess an *army numbardar.* Male Khan was in the 11th descending genaretion of Kunchoq Sharaptan, supposed to be the first settler of Wakha whose two sons were Labzong Gyalpo and Tumber Gyalpo. The latter became a Lama in a Monastery in Zanskar as per custom of the land, and later came to be known as Khushak Narichang in whose monastery an annual festival is still held wherein the Muslim as well as Buddhists of Lamas lineage participate regularly. Labzong Gyalpo fathered five sons Synigieh Gyalpo (the ruler of Stakche);Khri (pronounced as "thrii') Sulatan , (the ruler of Kartase); Gyaldecho (the ruler of Wakha) the fifth brother Zurgoo Ragocho died issueless used to live three months with each of his four brothers; being the youngest, he had no chance to marry and raise a family. Gyaldecho, the ruler of Wakha married but remained issueless. A Buddhist Lama told him that if he promises to give his first issue to Islam he will be blessed with a son and a son was born to him. The new born was instantly converted to Islam and was named Babar Khan who built a mosque at Wakha and brought a preacher from Zaddibal whose descendant, Sheikh Moosa was still the priest of the village when this study was conducted. A fort was built at Wakha ruins which are still a reminder of the old glory that it was. During the reign of Hashim Khan, the grandson of Babar Khan, Wakha was attacked by the Dogra General Zorawar Singh. Hashim Khan, was taken as a prisoner, first to Leh, then to Skardo where he died. Zorawar Singh ransacked and burnt the village monastery which has since been rebuilt on the ruins of the old one. Haji Khan, Azam Khan, Ghulam Khan and Ali Raza Khan held places in 5th, 4th, 3rd, and 2nd ascending generation respectively. Male Khan the present numbardar of Wakha is the son of Ali Raza Khan. The genealogy of Male Khan, collected from him and his first paternal cousin Ibrahim Khan, who is *up-sarpanch* of Wakha panchayat is furnished further :

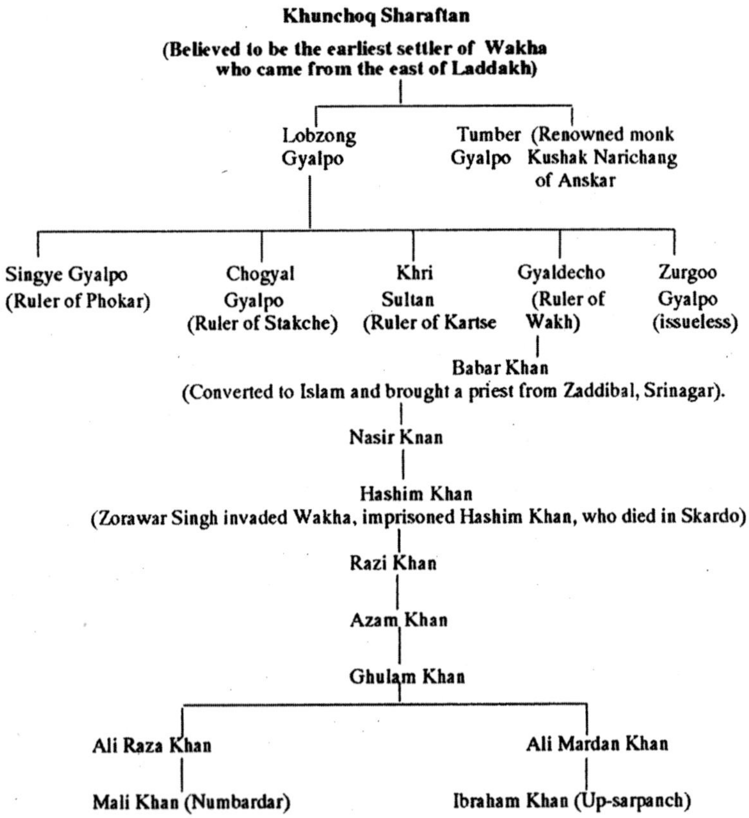

Genealogical diagram of the Numbardar of Wakha.

It is however, interesting to note that Male Khan holds the post of numbardar by virtue of his direct descent from the ruling lineage of Wakha whereas Ibrahim Khan, his father's brother's son seized an opportunity to become the *up-sarpanch* of Wakha panchayat through democratic processes.

Here it will be interesting to compare the two persons as the respective representative of the two systems feudal and democratic in terms of the authority and influence the two persons weild on the villagers of Wakha.

Mali Khan, a man in his sixties, was a mild person, equally respected by both Buddhist as well as Muslim populations of the village. He participated in the Buddhist as well as Muslim festivals equally and mixed with both sections of the village population with an equal ease. He was even alleged by the Muslims of Wakha to share *Chang*, the local beverage, of the Buddhists. Thus he became a target of many an accusing fingers of his Muslim bretheren. He married subsequently twice with Buddhist women from Lhasa, who were converted to Islam but failed to respond to Islamic way of covering the head with a scarf and observing namaz prayers. The Muslim section of the population, especially the elderly people protested against the liberal attitude of Male Khan but did not, somehow dare to open their mouths in front of him. Akhun Taqi, a priest of Wakha, even offered his son to the daughter of Male Khan if the latter adopts Islamic normative pattern but she refused to listen and Male Khan, when approached, declined to interfere in the affairs of his daughter who ultimately returned to her father. A case of criminal assault by Akhun Taqi was lodged in a court at Kargil by Male Khan but he remained stubborn not to go entirely by the Muslim system of values, perhaps he considered himself as the representative of the entire village but certainly not of a section of village population.

Ibrahim Khan on the other hand weilded much influence on the bureaucratic set up of Wakha as well as of Kargil. He was responsible for development activities taking place in the village. He was influential but not as popular as Male Khan. Ibrahim Khan got elected with the help of the bulk of Muslim votes and was somewhat alienated from the Buddhist population of the village with whom his interaction was seemingly limited. During on month of my stay at Wakha, he was never seen around any Buddhist household whereas Male Khan's daily schedule was to visit as many Buddhist as well as Muslim families of the village as posible. His presence was very much felt in the village whereas Ibrahim Khan was confined to a section of the village population. Though he was an elected representative of the village but certainly not an object of affection for the villagers as Male Khan was.

Motbar is selected by *numbardar* to assist him in his day to day functioning. The *numbardar* instructs him to procure wage labourers, to carry out necessary repairs if the village *Khul* is breached or blocked due to land slide. Like *numbardar,* the motbar is also exempted from army labour in border villges. In Hardas the number of *motbir* is one but in Wakha there are two Wazirs in lieu of *motbars* one Muslim and the other Buddhist. The tenure of *Motbar* or *Wazir* depends on the pleasure of *numbardar.* In border villages the traditional village council is constituted by the priests and *hajis* besides the numbardar and *motbar* hence assuming a more theocratic character but in Wakha the village *gopa* is more secular in character. Below the Wazirs, there are elected Kotwars one each representing Buddhist as well as Muslim population of the village. Below Kotwar Wakha gopa has four members;two Buddhist and two Muslim.

From the description furnished above two patterns of traditional political system emerge in Kargil as shown below:

Border villages Theocratic in political approach	Villages situated away from the border Secular in political approach
1. Karkit (Bare adalat : the court of elders) 2. Hardas (Gopa)	Wakha (Gopa)

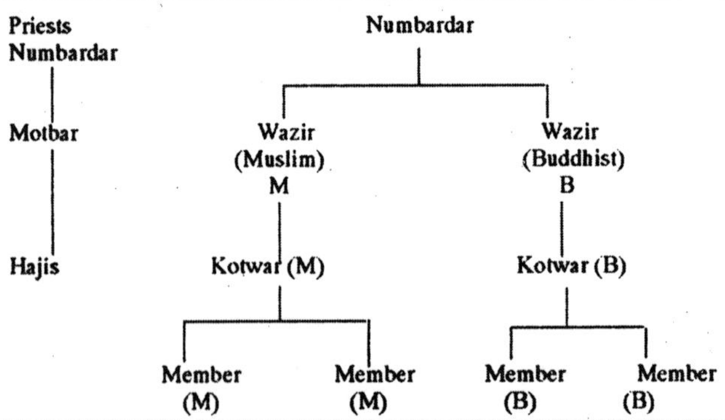

The above scheme shows that like other social institutions the political system in the border villages in highly tinged with and influenced by religion whereas the same proposition does not hold good in a peripheral village where Muslim population of Kargil merges with the Buddhist population which is significantly absent from the border villages of Hardas. The factor responsible for the people's reliance on religion especially in the border villages has given rise to ascendency to religo-political roles of the priest which will now be discussed in details in the pages to follow.

Role of Priests in Political Sysyem :

Since it is a well known fact that Islam is not merely a system of society but it claims to be complete social system wherein its followers perform various social roles assigned to them including political roles. This makes a priest's involvement essential in dealing with the disputes regarding marriage, divorce, desertion, inheritance of property, period of *Idda, mehr* and other aspects of muslim personal laws governed by *shariat.* The priests play an important role in case of an inter-village dispute. Once the villagers of Kargil and Hardas got embroiled in a dispute on *Kuhl.* The villgers of Karkit, being the earlier settlers feel aggrieved by the presence of the Baltis on the land which once belonged to them. The dispute between the two villages started with the digging of a *Kuhl* which was to start from the uplands of Karkit village and was to pass through Hardas. Initially, the residents of both the villages worked jointly for the project but when the said *Kuhl* was about to complete, the villagers of Karkit, especially of Majadas, raised objection over the passage of the canal through their lands. The matter was referred to the priests who forced the residents of Karkit and Hardas to reach to the following agreement a copy of which has been collected from the actual documents in possession of the respective parties. The agreement runs as follows:

"The necessity of writing this document arose from the dispute between the two villages on carving out a canal from Karkit rivers. The said dispute was even referred to the court of law. Having discussed the said problem thoroughly the elders and intellectuals of the two villages resolved the dispute with consensus in the light of the shariat on the following conditions :

(a) Head of new canal will be situated under the Karkit-choo bridge.

(b) Construction of any new canal above the proposed canal will not be allowed in future.

(c) The owners of land (whose land will come under the proposed canal) agreed on the proposed construction without any coercion.

(d) The inhabitants of Hardas and Karkit are entitled to irrigate their dry lands above or below the proposed canal.

(e) The inhabitants of Majdas and Karkit- choo are entitled to irrigate their dry lands from the proposed canal at appropriate place for three years from the date of this agreement.

(f) The agreed border between the two villages is as follows:

Half Birani Nala upto the Rajah's canal above and the hole in Zomtuq rock below in the middle of Birani Nala.

(g) The inhabitants of Karkit choo and Majdas are entitled to construct only canal upto the agreed border.

(h) The allocation of water will be according to the size of reclaimed land below the new proposed canal of Karkit choo, of Majadas and Hardas.

(i) The width of the canal will be 3 metres.

(j) The inhabitants of Majadas and Karkit-choo will have no right on Hardas canal after the stipulated period of three years irrigating their fields below the canal at Birani Nala.

(k) The compensation has been paid to the owners of land in Karkit-choo by the villagers of Hardas.

There are five copies of this agreement

(i) with the villagers of Hardas; (ii) with the villagers of Karkit-choo; (iii) with the villagers of Majadas (iv) with the government,duly stamped; (v) office of Madarsa-e-Islamia Kargil.

Dated : 13th Rajab, 1389 A.H.

Corresponding to September27, 1969.

The above is correct to the best of my knowledge signed (Sheikh Mohammad Ali - Hardas).

The agreement written above has been reached with the consent of the parties;

Sd/- Ahmad Husain.

Writer

Sd/- Mohammad Husain

The above is correct.

Sd/-Sheikh Mohammad Ali

In the name of Allah, this agreement has been reached after negotiations between Sheikh Mohammad Ali, Sheikh Hasan, Haji Akhun Ahmad Husain, and Sheikh Ali residents of Hardas.

AND

Ghulam Husain of Karkit -choo, who after giving considerable thoughts and safeguarding the interests of the residents of Karkit choo Majdas and Hardas, prepared this document. No one has a right to violate the provisions of this agreement.

Sd/-Ghulam Husain, Karkit choo.

The above agreement is the testimony of the power of dispute resolution enjoyed by the priestly class of Kargil. Inter- village disputes thus, are resolved by the priests to the people's satisfaction, even this dispute earlier could not be resolved by the traditional gopa of the two villages and the dispute was subsequently taken to the court of law.

The priestly class in Kargil is directly connected with the higher clerics of Shah Najaf, Karbala-e-Mualla (Iraq), Qum and Mashhad (Iran) from where they receive directions and advice for the people to follow those dictates.

Political affiliations : The Muslims of Kargil are divided between the ruling National Conference and the main opposition Congress. One of the priests of Kargil is the nominated member of the State Legislative Council. Whenever a VIP visits Kargil, the villagers are informed to participate in political rallies (Jalsa) at Kargil where they go as detached observers, listen the speeches and discuss the proceedings of the meeting briskly after they return to their respective villages. The Kargil Muslims have a tendency to look at India for their political inspirations as one of the informants had put.

"Thank God : We are living in " Jamhooriat". The God is above and Sarkar below. Our crops come up due to the kindness of Allah and the Sarkar gives us free rations. There is none else to bank upon".

The residents of the adjoining hamlets of Haral Badgam of Karkit village liberated during 1971 war between India and Pakistan were rather vague about the political processes at work just a few yards away from their hamlets. When they were asked as who is your leader. Only few of them could say "Indira Saheb". When asked about the change that resulted after liberation of the illegally occupied hamlets a resident of the libarated hamlets said,

"Under the old rule, only the rich people could go to Skardo for making their purchases. Today even the poorest of the poor amongst us can go to Kargil with a load of fuelwood and by selling wood he can ensure a meal to his children. Formerly we depended for our necessities on the mercy of the Tehsildar who would bring sugar and salt for distribution. He would come only during the summers and his visits too were irregular. Only Allah knows how we survived. Our main source of earning was supply of fuel wood to the enemy's forces who paid us 4/- for the day's labour but there was nothing to bank upon during winters".

The political structure of the liberated hamlets was only in the skeletal form. Only one numbardar used to look after both the illegelly occupied hamlets. Priestly class could also not be found in the said hamlets. The people were the worst sufferers as many of the residents went to places of pilgrimage and could not return to their homes after the end of hostility. They had never participated in any election nor voted for any one of their representatives unlike their neighbourers who had undergone successive general election and were fully aware of the power of adult franchise. Political awareness dawns through wide participation in political processes and spread of education; the residents of the occupied hamlets were deprived of both. Nearly for a quarter of a century of enemy's illegal occupation of the two hamlets, there was no sign of even a primary school for the people living under the illegal occupation. That was the fate of the so called "Azad Kashmiris". The people of Haral and Haral Begdam were neither 'Azad' under the illegal rulers nor could they join the processes of development ushered in the state of Jammu and Kashmir since the instruments of Accession were signed between erstwhile rulers and the Government of India.

CHAPTER VII

THE BALTI SOCIAL SYSTEM - CONTINUITY AND CHANGE

There is a general impression in Laddakh that the Balti are a static monolith encradled in the ecological insulation and theocratic dogmatism. No society can manage to be static on its own volition. Trends of change are visible among the Balti both at micro and macro perspectives. The former are visible in the traits of their culture and the latter in their historical past.

Changes in Balti Culture :

The process of change in the Balti culture are neither unilineal nor sequential. The direction of change suggests three levels of change enumerated below :

1. Continuity of Cultural Traits :

The cultural traits indicating continuity, contrary to earlier sociolgical propositions, fall, under the category of material culture: housing pattern, house types, dress pattern, ornamentation, food habits, an absolute renunciation of the Buddhist brew *chang*. Ecomomic activities too changed considerably; the deficient agriculture supplements with the itinerant trade gave rise to labour combination in the last fifty years. Traditional village council *Goba* too remained intact with peripheral changes.

2 Change and Equilibrium :

The life-cycle rituals and an alteration of the annual calender of fairs and festivities suggest and attempt to adjust after transition from the Buddhist past to the Islamic present. Wakha shows a compromise and equilibrium in sharing the traditional as well as recently emerging political powers in the region. The numberdar of Wakha, a hereditary head of the traditional Village council, appoints two Wazirs to assist him, one belonging to the Buddhist segment of the village population and the other from the Muslim of the village. Similarly, other offices of the Goba two each are appointed from the two segments of the village population. The Buddhist *amchi*, medicineman, too provides succour to the willing Muslim brethern of the village.

3. Matters of faith, customary laws, an absolute renunciation of polyandry suggest an absolute departure from the Buddhist past to the Islamic present. Muta system, with greater flexibilty than the marriage (*nikah-e-deaimi*) came into vogue as an adujstability measure but the recent trends show a greater inclination towards permanent marriage contracts.

The trends of chage in the Balti social system, as indicated earlier, are contrary to theory of 'culture lag' wherein changes in material culture are faster than those occuring at ideational and non-material traits. Ecology helped to maintain a continuity in material culture where the ideology of the group has witnessed various changes from time to time which may be termed as various phases of transition from Bonism to Buddhism, Buddhism to Islam; from the Dogra subjecthood to the Indian citizenship and subsequent Pakistani attack on their territories in 1947,1965, and 1971. A large chunk of the people 's territory came under the illegal occupation of Pakistan. The latest wave of changes were ushered in after Kargil was thrown open to tourists and was accorded the status of a district with two sub-divisions, Kargil and Zenskar.

Islam brought about major changes in rules of marriage, inheritance,succession, religious tenets and rituals. Food habits, dress and ornamentation, traditional political system, economic organisation,house types, traditional fairs and festivals have undergone only through peripheral changes until Pakistan came into being and international borders were closed. This caused a considerable change in economic activities. Trade as a major sorce of livelihood came to an abrupt end and hordes of Baltis started moving out of their habitats in search of wage labour to various parts of Himachal Pradesh, Uttar Pradesh and other neighbouring areas. Subsequently, some of the Balti settlements emerged around Nainital and Dehradun districts of Uttar Pradesh. The economic conditions witnessed an improvement and their incomes improved considerably. Newly acquired capital gains were subsequently recycled to strengthen religious beleifs and ideology by way of sending young boys to the Islamic centres of learning situated in Iraq and Iran for advanced training in Islamic *fiqah* (jurisprudence). This new breed of scholars returned to their respective villages fully armed with the capacity to lead to the people to the path of righteousness'. A greater attention was also paid to strengthen the local ***madarsahs*** which produce the priests of the lower order.

After Kargil was declared open for tourist's traffic followed by a faster and hectic pace of planned development, an effective network of roads and communication was established. Secular education, medi-care, and successive exercises in adult franchise resulted into melting the ice of seclusion and covert self-perception giving rise to a better understanding of the prevailing situations and better interaction with the segments of Indian population. They look towards India for all succour they require and are always keen to get justice within the framework of the Indian Constitution. They have kept a constant liasion with the places of theological leararning situated at Lucknow and Varanasi. They have largely remained immuned and indifferent to the ongoing turmoil ravaging the valley of Kashmir, though, majority of their kin remain trapped in the illegally occupied areas across the Line of Actual Control. The fissiperous propaganda blitz from across the borders has left very little impression on them. The flourishing tourist industry in Kargil has turned many of them into successful hotliers and guides to those afflicted with the lure of some of the mightiest Himalyan peaks situated in Kargil. The extent of politicisation of religion remains at the lowest levels in Kargil in comparison to other parts of the State.

The national media has an element of exaggeration in highlighting religious polarisation among the local Muslims and Buddhist populations but very few scribes know that the Balti of Wakha village still contribute their mite in organising the annual festival at the monastery dedicated to and built by Kushak Narichang who is the common ancestor of many a villagers of Wakha-both Buddhists as well as Muslim. The Muslim Baltis of Wakha not only contribute but atttend the said fair in person and are looked after well by the management of the said monastery. They are supplied with the meat (slaughtered by a muslim) and dry rations during the festival. The creation of Laddakh Buddhist Association and Laddakh Muslim Association (LAMA) might have helped in the process of alienation between the two communities but this divsive tendency is confined to the two cities,i.e., Leh and Kargil. The rural population has been able to maintain the cultural pluralism for which Laddakh is well known for ages. This divisive tendency can be effectively curbed if both the districts as a whole are declared as Tribal Districts instead of declaring a few selected ethnic groups as Scheduled Tribe for a uniform and an indescriminate development. This action would leave all sections of population with fewer complaints against differentiation and selective bias.

The people's tolerant behaviour seems to be an outcome of their past Buddhist legacy wherein militancy has a little place. The religious polarisation visible is only skin-deep and is mainly being instigated by political forces which try to maintain their sway over the masses but the Laddakhi demand for a status of Union Territory accorded to the region is very much within the consititutional framework and is negotiable. This demand too is a result of centuries of autocratic rule, sheer neglect of Laddakhi aspirations, and a reflection of the people's desire to join the Indian mainstream. The Balti have stoutly refused to be a part of the secessionist and isolationist forces roasting their goose in other parts of the State. For keeping their hearth of communal inferno silent, the people of Ladakh in general and the Balti in particular have done a commendable job. They could do so because of a higher degree of conformity to their religious tenets which teach of *ahimsa,* mutual love, peaceful co-existence, extolling the virtues of all religions and giving up place to coercion in religious matters of no religion on earth teaches violence, haterd, killing arson, militany and dogmatism. The spirit of Bulbul Shah who saw the elements for faith written on the face and of paganism(*kufr*) in plait of hair of Rinchin Bhot, who according to the saint, held both Islam and Paganisms in his fists, the cynosure of beholders.The two remained friends until death seperated them. Almost each village in eastern Kargil has seen the existence of a Buddhist monastery (*gompa*) and a *matamsara* or a mosque side by side through the centuries. Laddhak appears to be the strongest bastion of secularism and it may be hoped that the coming decades will not see any change in the situation.

THE ALCHEMY OF COMMUNALISM IN LADDAKH

India is passing through the trauma of communal frenzy. In this grim scenario Laddakh stands out as a shining example of amity, mutul co-existence and mutual understanding for various religious faiths. The Balti, while sefeguarding their own system of beliefs do not denigrate other faiths. Positive secularism is inherent in their social system. The peasantry is the bastion of secularism and communal hatred is the characteristic of the Urban political elite who do not spare any effort to influence the peasantry by their money and muscle power, allurements and coercion. The spreading network of communication, press, film and electronic media act as catalyst to complete the process as mentioned in the following diag :

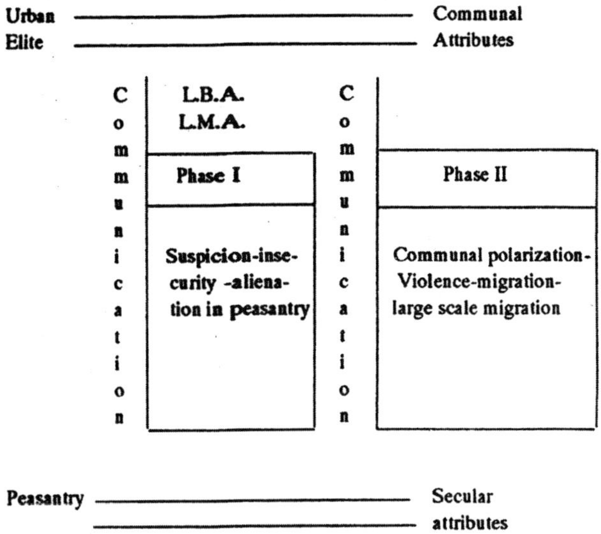

LaddakhBuddhist Association (L.B.A.) and LaddakhMuslim Association (L.M.A.) are speare-heading their respective campaigns for a Buddhist Leh and Muslim Kargil. The catchy slogan are reaching to the peasantry of Laddakh through electronic media and the press and creating a sense of suspicion and insecurity among the peasantry but the Laddakhi peasantry was sound enough to absorb the initial shoks of politically motivated Communalism. If sincere efforts are not made to stem the rot, the alienation is bound to result into communal holocaust with the concomittant results of migration, regimentation and ultimately civil war fuelled by the internal communal forces and external scessionists elements. In this grim scenario the Buddhist and Muslims of Laddakh should be encouraged and be provided with all necessary inentives to resolve their outstanding problems themselves with the least interference by the outside forces. The entry of Communal activists in the garb of tourists to Ladakh should be curbed and controlled effectively by the state intelligence agencies, the renowned citizens of the area and sociallly conscious political leaders who are committed to uphold and strengthen the inherent and inbuilt secularism in Indian society. Various media too have a responsibility towards building and strengthening the Indian nationhood in general and of Laddakh in particular. Let us have a look at the role played by the by Doordarshan under Himalaya Ki Khoj. The serials were informative, interesting and entertaining but they woefully lacked the social objectivity. None of the serials under the above title deal with Kargil which predominantly contains Muslim population of the Dard and Balti. They have failed to uncover the mechanism of equilibrium that the people of Laddakh have evolved over the centuries in order to keep their Ladakhi identity intact. Will not it be interesting to talk about the builder of a mosque in Shey monastery near Leh ? Are not they aware of the obeisance paid by the Balti and Argon to their late Buddhist ancestors ? Many a romantic stories may be woven around the cases of frequent conversion in Laddakh from one faith to another as a result of love marriages, famines or maltreatment of individuals within the realm of families. The electronic media suffers with the lack of consciousness about the integrative meachanism built in the Laddakhi society. They have avoided to go into the depth of folk- lores and folk songs of the Laddakhi people which incapasulates many a hidden mechanism of cultural pluralism which the people of Ladakh have so assiduously preserved and guarded until now. A sojourn into the depth of Laddakhi culture by the electronic media is the need of the day. A superficial portrayal of culture does immense damage to the peoples' cultural susceptibilities and adds the fuel to the inferno of the communal hatred. Over emphasis on one group of people creates a sense of neglect and deprivation in another group.

The press and film media could do wonders witn the available sufficient material to promote cultural integration in Laddakh. They should go to the people directly and come out with the peoples' version of happenings.They may observe and investigate the life and inspiration of young apprentice *chomos* (nuns) of the age varying between eight to eighty years who pass their lives in the dark chambers of a monastery or the young Balti and Argon boys who are coerced to join the local *madarasahs* for lessons in theology. The journalism in Laddakh cannot but be a sort of ethno journalism protraying the lives of the people, their grim battle for survival, the limitations of development planning imposed by ecology, nepotism and corruption and its impact on the poorest of the poor like the Champa, Gara, Bada and Mon. The journalism in Laddakhas got to be socially meaningful, positive and constructive.

GLOSSARY OF LOCAL TERMS

Aaq	to disown
Aba	a black tunic don by priests. Also a term of address for father
Arbaeen	synonym to Nishuniz
Ache	elder sister
Agha	Saiyid
Ahadis	plural of *hadis* (tradition)
Ahle-bait	member of the Prophet Mohammad's house-hold.
Akhun	priest- cum-medicineman
Alam	a replica of the standard of Imam Husain
Aloo	Potatoes
Aima	Balti term of address for mother
Amama	a round cap worn by a priest
Amchis	Buddhist medicineman
Amo	term of reference for mother's sister
Ana	mother's brother's wife
Ansaar	close companion
Apa	a term of reference for father's father and mother's father
Aqeeqa	obligatory shaving of the child's head
Ashepa/daq-pa	term of reference for husband
Asho	term address for daughter's husband
Ashoor	the 10th day of Moharram

Ata	a term of reference for father or father's brother
Athar	handle
Azaab	super natural curse
Bakhstan/Kash	negotiated marriage
Baq-pa	bride-groom
Baq-ma	bride
Baradin	a local festival
Barangghuduns	flagellating of breast
Biryani	fried rice seasoned with mutton
Bokhari	a heating device/a guest room
Brangshrik	pendant
Brugma	harvesting operation
Burjing	inferior variety of land
Cha	tea
Chagsi-gapa	kotwal
Chagsot	treasurer
Chaharda masoomin	the fourteen innocents i.e. Prophet Mohammad,his daughter Fatima and twelve Imams
Chakmak	a devise used for making fire
Chaksha	laterine
Chang	a popular drink in Laddakh
Chapakli	a neclace worn by Balti women
Chari	a rough woollen beadstead made of goat wool
Chas	kitchen garden
Chasis-pa	close associates and friends of the groom
Chas-saagzar	land used for kitchen garden
Chaugan	horse-polo
Chempopa	tailor
Chilishtie	members of bride-groom's party
Chilla	40th day of the death
Chimeh	a cremonial feast given by the bride groom's father to his kin before marriage
Chinan	break fast

Chudeh	a marriage ceremony
Chuli	apricots
Chyut	second crops
Dahun	head-scarf
Dari	carpet
Das	plain
Dastar-khan	a cloth spread whereupon meals are served
Datso	mediator
Dawa	medicines
Dewankhana	guest house/ante-chamber
Djinn	genii
Donro	a digging stick made of wood and iron
Dorma	trousers made of wool
Dua	prayer
Dua-e-khair	prayer for the well being of the community
Durpo	raddish
Espumet	winnowing
Fajir	morning prayers
Fasal-ka-sadqa	a post-harvest festival
Fateha	a death ritual performed on the third and fortieth days
Finjaan	dainty cups in which qahwa is served
Fitra/zakaat-e-badni	a levy paid on the day of Id-ul-fitr
Fungra	a room on the first floor used for storing fodder
Furo-e-din	branches of religions
Geluk-pa	yellow cap seat
Ghadir-e-khum	a place in Saudi Arabia
Ghusl	bath
Ghusl-e-istahaza	purificatory bath performed after discharge of menstrual blood
Ghusl-e-maiyat	funerary bath
Ghusl-e-mas-e-maiyat	purificatory bath taken by a person who has touched a corpse

Ghusl-e-nifaas	purificatory bath on the fortieth day after child birth
Goba	traditional panchayat
Gobhi	cabbage
Gonyal	a room on the ground floor used for keeping cows and yaks
Gopa	the traditional village council
Gosh-sakhanej	kitchen-cum-living room
Granz-/zyot	a room on the first floor used for storing victuals
Grim	naked barley
Gropyngyal/fungra	a room of the first floor used for storing fodder
Gungli	millet
Gur-gur	a vessel in which tea is prepared
Gur-gur-cha	tea prepared with green tea-leves in boiling water,by mixing salt,soda and butter
Gyalpo/kahlon	small province with partial independence
Hadith	tradition
Haiya-ala-khairal amal	a portion of azaan as prevalent amal among the Balti Shias
Haiya-ala-khairal-bashar	a portion of azaan as prevalent among the Nurbakhashi.
Hajala	the practice wherein a divorced woman marries another men and seeks a decree of divorce in order to remarry with the man divorced earlier
Haji	one who has performed the Haj pilgrimage but the Balti call Haji to one who has returned after the pilgrimage of the mazaars of various Imams and other family members of the Prophet Mohammad
Hal	plough
Halpa	mediator
Halwa	pudding
Hardoqpi ta:viz	the charm that is burnt and the ashes are smeared on eyes to cure opthamological disorders

Hawk	a leafy vegetable popular among the Kashmiri
Hinjung	the household established by a married person who has abdicated Lamahood
Hinna	myrtle paste
Id	a festival
Id-e-qurban	the festival celebrated to commemorate the sacrifice of the Prophet Ismael to Allah by the Prophet Abraham.
Idda	a prescribed period of abstinence from marriage
Ijtihad	a high degree awarded in theistic learning
Ilm-e-ramal	the science pertaining to the divination
Imaan	moral character and conviction
Imambara	an enclosure wherein religious congregation other than Namaz prayers are held.
Imam-e-waqt	the Twelfth Imam Al Mahdi
Iman	conviction
Irbazdus	thirteenth day of Moharram
Ishnanmizaan	feast at night in the honour of the bride's relations
Jahannum/dozakh	the hell
Jalsa	political meeting
Ja-namaaz	a carpet on which namaz is performed
Jehad	an effort or striving
Jing-changet	ploughing
Jinchotang	irrigation
Kache-pa	Kashmiri
Kah-dam	a purer Buddhist Model
Kakatadsi	master of the house
Kanak	wheat
Kari	a water container made of copper or aluminium
Karpo-chuli	white apricots
Kotwar	an office in traditional village council
Kalbur	goat skin bags

Ketli	kettle
Khachi	a paste prepared from parched barley flour
Khak-e-shifa	the earth of Karbala which is believed to possess certain therapeutic qualities
Khandaan	family
Khansgo	feast
Kharpons	commander of forts
Khatna	circumcission
Khinchan	ornaments containing charms or verses from holy Quran
Khiuskoret	granary
Khoi	cap
Khrumpons	magistrate
Khums	an obligatory levy paid by every Balti individual
Khuftan	marriage performed secretly
Kohlon	district officer
Koral	cups made of china clay
Kuhl	aquaduct
Kurtani	a shirt (unsewed)
Lafzan	a type of sweet pudding made of butter
Lattoo	a type of mine
Lo	term of address for either of the two spouse
Lha-khang	small tample
Liptoncha	sweetened tea
Lonpos	governors of towns
Lota	vessel
Madarasah	school where religius teachings are imparted
Mahr	the guarantee money paid by the groom's side to the parents of the bride
Maja	middle
Majlis	religious congregation commemerating the martyredom in Karbala
Makpa	marriage by service
Makpons	commander-in-chief

Mal-e-Imam	a share of Khums given to the deputies of Imam
Mal-e-sadat	a portion of Khums levy given to the Saiyid
Ma-moon	one who perform the prayer under the guidance of Imam
Marsia	tragic dirges
Marsia-khani	recitation of dirges
Masir	kins related through the mother
Matamsara/Imam-bara	an enclosure wherein religious congregations pertaining to Moharram and other occasions take place
Me	term of address for husband in Wakha
Member-e-Rasul	the replica of the Prophet Mohammad's pulpit
Mipons/gopas	head man of the village
Mistri	artisans
Momo	mother's brother
Mome	companion
Mongur	a cup made of copper and polished from within with a coat of lead
Motbar	assistant to the head man
Motugizan	lunch
Muazzin	the caller for prayers
Mujtahid	clergy/priest/deputy
Mulaq	turnips
Muljing	a type of land situated near the irrigation sources
Mutah	temporary marriage contract
Naade-Ali	semi-precious stones on which the sacred verse of Naad-e-Ali are inscribes
Nacha	an ornament made of small beads of silver
Nahi-an-al-munkir	path of righteousness
Namaz	prayers
Namaz-e-asr	prayer performed in afternoon but before the sun set

Namaz-e-Id	special prayers on the day of Id
Namaz-e-isha	prayer performed in the evening but before mid-night
Namaz-e-janaza	prayar performed for a dead body before a burial
Namaz-e-magrib	praver performed 15 minutes after sun-set
Namaz-e-zohar	mid-day prayers
Nas	grim
Nating	skull-cap made of wool
Nauha-khani	lamentation
Navroz	the Persian New Year Day
Nazar	offering
Nazari	a local festival/sacrifice
Nikah	a marriage ritual
Nikah-e-daimi	permanent marriage contract
Nikah-e-inqatai	temporary marriage contract (muta)
Nosh-yoni	a ceremonial bath undertaken by the mother after seven days of delivery
Numberdar	village head man
Ol	grass land
Paak	clean
Pandop	a disk like silver ornament worn by married women
Panjotra	a system of collection of revenue
Paposh	footwear
Pasham	a special type of wool
Pattoo	woollen cloth woven locally
Phaphi	a term of reference for mother's brother as to in father's sister
Pharali	share
Phasir	agnates
Pheonle	spade
Phizbezan	dinner
Phogon	spoons made of aluminium

Phosphon	an agnatic kin group, members of which trace their descent from a male common ancestor
Phril	male member of second descending generation
Potriksh	people of pot
Qaasida	poems eulogising the qualities of the Prophet Mohammad and his descendants
Qahwa	a beverage
Qibla	the direction for namaz prayers
Qaba	gown
Quran-khani	the recitation of the holy Quran
Ranthogtoget	grinding
Rezm	a container for keeping flour
Rinthe	mahr
Rogra	an enclosure for keeping sheep
Roza	thirty days of fasting in the ninth month of the Islam calender
Roza-shikani	fast-breaking feast
Sa/sum	pre-mature melting of snow through an artificial device
Sajda	prostration
Sakpa	a piece of leather cover the back; mainly used by women while carrying baskets
Salini	a piece of cloth
Sam	ice
Samawar	a kettle like utensil
Sanad	letter of the appointment
Sando	a lion cloth covering body from abdomen to feat
Sattoo/sattu	flour of parched barley
Sawab	merit
Schendebf	marriage by exchange
Schewet	barley being roasted in iron vessels by heating it with sand
Schumet	harvesting operation

Seerat	a sermon enumerating the personal qualities of Prophet Mohammad and his close kin
Segha	recitation of holy verses at the time of marriage
Sheb-e-aashoora	the eve of Ashoora, the 10th day of Moharram
Shaglo	stonedisk
Shahadatnama	witness testifying the good conduct of the deceased
Shakshi-raaj	autocratic rule
Shalba	sowing
Shanma	peas
Shara	Islamic code of conduct
Shilling-khyang	a room used for storing fuel
Shogumpa	provincial collectors of taxes and customs
Slum	ceremonial feast
Sajdagah	a disk on which head is placed while performing sajda during namaz
Skarkus	girdle
Skiu	butter
Skut-pa	kin related through wife
Slaap	land-slides
Saah	barley
Saget	farmer
Surah	a Quranic verse
Swell-veyas	to capture a bride
Taapti-ta-viz	a charm which is worn either as a necklace or as an armlet for curing mental discorders
Tabbaq/tabaq	plates plates made of copper
Tabraarruk	refreshment
Taimum	dry bath with dust
Takche	a pointed dibble made of iron
Talaq	divorce
Tasbih-e-fatima	rosary
Ta:viz	charm

Tha-jing	land situated away from the village on the hill near the flowing rivers
Thangmi-ta-viz	charm that is soaked in water and the water is administred to a patient suffering from body and toothaches
Thaqskan	weaver
That	a carf covering the head
Thazan	a feast
Thog	first crop
Thoma	shoe of a plough
Tozar	refreshment
Tro/Kanak	wheat
Tsampa	barley flour
Tso-ke-khyut	processing
Tumar	ornament studded with semiprecious stones
Turumba/gangni	millets
Up-sarpanch	an officer in the statutory village council
Urdingu	bangles
Usool-e-din	the guiding principles of Islam
Wajib	compulsory prayers
Wakil	witnesses
Wazir	assistant to numberdar
Wazu	obluations
Waggu	mat
Yas-khuan	ploughing
Yo	barley
Yurma/yurmaba	weeding
Zakaat	an obligatory levy
Zamidar	tillers of the soil
Zar-zarbroq	a childlike hilly feature in Wakha
Zho/zhomo	a mixed bread of yak or cow
Zho	mother's brother's son, daughter's son,son' and brother's son
Zhona	father's brother's daughter
Zongse/Bustring	the term of reference to wife

Bibliography

Ah-luwalia,H.P.S.	1980	*Hermit kingdom- Ladakh*, Delhi: Vikas.
Baker,P.T.	1978	*Biology of High Altitude people* Cambridge: University press
Cunningham, Alexander	1970	*Ladakh Physical,Statistical and Historical.* New Delhi : Sagar Publications.
Drew, Fredrick	1875	*Jummoo and Kashmir Territories A Geographical account.* London: Edward Stanford.(Reprint 1971)
Firth,Raymond	1969	"Capital, Saving and Credit in Peasant Societies _ A view point from Economic Anthropology" in *Capital, Saving and Credit in Peasant Societies.* Ed. by Raymond Firth and B.S. Yamey.London: George Allen and Unwin
Gazetteer of Kashmir and Ladakh	1974	(Originally 1890). Delhi : Vivek Publishing House (Reprint)
Hashmatul-lah,Moulvi	1939	*Mukhtasar Tarikh-e-Jammu* (Urdu).Lucknow: Nawal Kishore
Hasan, Mohibbul	1959	*Kashmir Under the Sultans.* Iran Society

Hughes, T.P.	1885	*Dictionary of Islam*. New Delhi : Cosmo Publication : Reprinted in 1977
Polanyi, Karl	1957	"The economy as Instituted Process" in *Trade and Market in the Early Empires*, Glencoe:Illinois; The Free Press
Rizvi, B.R.	1974	"Social Stratification in Western Himalayas A Comparative Study of Bodhs of Spiti and Muslims of Kargil " *Bulletin*, Anthropological Survey of India. Vol. NO. XXIII, No. 1-2 pp- 20-33
	1977	"Ecology and Nomadism : A study of some migrating groups of Ladakh" in *Nomadism in India*. Ed. P.K.Mishra and K.S.Malhotra. Calcutta : Anthropological Survey of India and Indian Statistical Institute
	1987	"Class formation and conflict in a Polyandrous Village of Himachal Pardesh" In The *Himalyan Heritage!*.ed. M.K. Raha. Delhi : Gyan Publishing House.
Zaidi, Qari Syed Ali Main	1965	*Aina-e-Haqiqat Bajaw ab-e-Inkishaf-e-Haqiqat;*Lucknow : Idara-e-Babul Qloom.
Zutshi, J.N. (ed)	1970	Census of India, 1961 Vol. VI ,Part VI, No. 13 Jammu and Kashmir Village Survey Monograph of Kharboo (Tehsil Kargil, District Ladakh) Delhi : Manager of Publications.

INDEX

1. A Vertically Extended Family sitting in front of Village Mosque

2. A young Balti Girl

3. A young Balti Mourner on Ashura-10th Moharram

4. A contingent of young boys mourning on 10th Moharram

5. A Balti Kitchen is a Family Sitting Room

6. Roasting grim to be ground into Khache

7. Women actively participate in all agricultural activities

8. An elderly balti Woman with her ornaments

9. The Village landscape

10. A Balti Summer house

11. Settlement pattern

12. Occupational specialization is an achieved status

13. The village Baker's shop

14. Returning home after the day's chores

15. A stall for free distribution of Sharbat (Sabeel) on 10th Moharram

16. "I am less alone when I am alone"-A young Balti Girl

17. Ladakh in Flux

18. The Balti Attending a Budhist Festival - a group of Bedas with their Musical instruments sitting in the background

19. Flat Roof-top of the Balti House with Chimney and drying tufts of leafy Vegetables left for drying

20. Zar-Zar Broq : The Growing Mountain near Wakha

21. Siblings at Play